# INSIGHT: The Substance and Rewards of Teaching

## HERBERT KOHL

**Addison-Wesley Publishing Company**
Menlo Park, California     Reading, Massachusetts
London     Amsterdam     Don Mills, Ontario     Sydney

D1343683

JEANETTE MOSS, CLAUDIA COHL,
AND ALL THE OTHER PEOPLE I WORKED WITH
AT *TEACHER MAGAZINE*

**This book is published by the Addison-Wesley Innovative Division.**

Book design: Rodelinde Albrecht

ISBN-0-201-04407-2
ABCDEF-ML-898765432

# A Prefatory Note

There are several ways to approach this book. One is simply to read it straight through and then to return to sections that have suggestions you want to incorporate into your classroom program. Another way to begin is with a topic that is of particular interest to you such as writing or environmental studies, and read through and test some of the material in the section that focuses on that topic. Finally, you can begin with a particular subsection that may have immediate use because of current work in your classroom.

In order to encourage these different ways of approaching the text the table of contents includes a short summary of each subsection in the book and it would make sense to begin the book by reading through these summaries. Though much of the material here originated in articles I wrote for *Teacher Magazine*, all the material has been rewritten. Some articles have been merged with others, some recast. There is also material from articles that never got published as well as material appropriate to the extended discussion of issues and techniques that is hard to include in a short column but possible in book form. I tried to shape this book as a whole, independent of the columns in which many of its ideas were originally expressed, to share what I believe are some valuable insights I've picked up over the last 20 years of teaching. This book is a reaffirmation of what has been at the core of all my articles for *Teacher Magazine*: that the teaching of young people is a wonderful life that is essential to the survival of democracy and the enrichment of the lives of the young.

# Contents

# Introduction

From 1968 to 1980, January, September, and May each signalled a new yearly cycle for me. January is when everyone celebrates the New Year; September is the beginning of the new year for us teachers; and May is the month I completed my column for the September issue of *Teacher Magazine*. I learned to live with the irony of welcoming teachers back to school when I was not quite done with my own teaching year. In March of 1981, I was informed that *Teacher Magazine* would not publish again; that some corporate decisions resulted in the elimination of a magazine that had addressed teachers for over a hundred years. The main reasons given were inflation, a current disillusion with public education that discourages advertisers, and declining school enrollment with only 25% of our adult population having school age children.

I missed writing down thoughts on teaching every month especially now that creative teaching needs all the support it can get. Fortunately, *Learning Magazine* asked me to write features for them and so it is still possible to reach people serious about teaching in a time when one wonders how many people are serious about our children. These are not easy times for teachers who are trying to do decent work in the public schools. The excitement of the sixties and the hard work of the seventies to create student-oriented excellent classroom practice has been replaced by depression and demoralization. Budget cuts and demands for an impoverished contentless so-called basic skills curriculum have damaged many excellent programs. Nevertheless, the children are still there with the same needs, and ideas that are pushed aside because of political pressure are not invalid simply because they are under attack. There is perhaps no more important time to reaffirm commitment to creative teaching and the empowerment of students than times like these when the goals of decent education and equal opportunity for all children are in danger.

I was delighted when the Innovative Division of Addison-Wesley suggested the idea of updating and organizing a collection of my over 100

*Teacher* columns and articles. It was an opportunity to sort out the best of my past work, to add new ideas and techniques, and most importantly, to remind myself and other teachers of the excitement and importance of keeping on teaching and sustaining our concern for young people.

There are many pressures we all feel to give up teaching creatively and to subject ourselves and our students to ideas and methods we don't believe in. It is also easy to find reasons to give in and develop excuses to subordinate thought and creativity to obedience and conformity. It's important to realize that these pressures are not new. For the past 15 years I have been trying to encourage teachers to open things up in their schools, to make their classrooms livable, to create choices for their students. Some teachers have been overtly hostile and closed to the kinds of change I've suggested. Others have been excited and enthusiastic about trying new things. Some have been making changes for years and have found support in the recent writing on the subject.

The great majority of teachers I have spoken with, however, are interested in the idea of openness but are still unwilling to try it in their own classrooms. These teachers acknowledge that school is frequently irrelevant and often oppressive for student and teacher alike. Yet they claim that change must be sanctioned from above or supported outside of the public schools. Here are some of the excuses teachers have given to justify not changing:

1. I can't change because my principal won't let me. Variations on this theme are: The other teachers won't like what I'm doing; the janitor thinks my classroom is too messy; the school secretaries object to the noise in my room.

2. I can't change because I'm afraid. This general expression of fear has many manifestations and is perhaps the most common excuse given. Some teachers are afraid that they won't know what to do in an open situation where they give up their absolute power. Others are afraid that they'll lose their jobs or be forced to confront their supervisors. Some teachers are afraid that their students might go wild and hurt them if controls were removed, or that the students might say unpleasant truths about them.

3. I can't change because the parents won't understand. Teachers are afraid that they will get static from the parents of their students, that the parents will want to defend a rigidly structured form of learning and that they won't understand the values of an open classroom.

4. I can't change because open learning will harm my students in their future schooling because the next year they will have to return to the old rigid system. A variation on this argument goes that students in

open classrooms might be happier but they won't be prepared to get into college and that is an unfair disadvantage for the student.

5. I can't change because the time isn't ripe, because the political climate in my community opposes change.

The five categories of excuses overlap considerably, and the fear of change is present in all of them. The fact that so many teachers feel compelled to make excuses is a positive phenomenon, for it means that they perceive the need to change even if their role in creating change isn't clear. I will examine the five categories and suggest ways in which teachers can move from excuses to actions.

*My principal won't let me change.* Independent adults don't need permission to change their personal ways of living. Teachers rarely feel or act independently insofar as their school lives are concerned. Only recently have the union and teachers' associations begun to make demands in the name of teachers. Teachers usually follow directions, take what is given them and live lives of quiet frustration in their classrooms.

I know a teacher who tried to open up her room by moving the chairs around and letting the students sit where they wanted. The janitor in the school complained to the principal that her new arrangement made his job of cleaning the room more difficult, and the principal ordered the teacher to put the desks back in rows and columns for the convenience of the janitor.

The teacher complied and complained to me that she wanted badly to open up her room but the principal wouldn't let her. I asked her why she didn't fight his decision. After all, the principal knew as well as she did that schools do not exist to make janitors' jobs easier. She just shrugged. She didn't want trouble. Yet she had trouble anyhow. She lived with her frustration and it was communicated to her students. When I visited the room I could sense defeat.

She could have fought reasonably and well over the placement of tables and desks in her room. She could have continued her arrangement and straightened out the desks before the janitor arrived to clean. But she wasn't used to acting on her own, to taking initiative and defending what she believed was right. She was part of the silent majority of teachers who want to change but are so used to being dependent on the school system to make decisions for them that they don't know how to act independently.

Many changes can take place through the initiative of individual teachers. After all, how much does a supervisor know of what actually happens in the classroom? There are some innovations that can only be carried out with permission since they are so visible. Taking four trips a week, or extending the boundaries of one's classroom into the halls, or painting the walls of the schools are such public acts that they will attract immediate attention. But providing students with time to do what they care to, developing a series of activities that the students can choose to participate in, putting down rugs in corners of the classroom, seeing students before nine and after three o'clock are much less conspicuous ways of beginning to open things up. No attempt to change is without risk, however. This leads to the second category of excuses.

*I can't change because I'm afraid.* Many teachers live with fears all their professional lives. The more rigid a classroom the more the teacher generally fears the students. When a great distance is maintained between teacher and students it is natural that mutual fears develop. The students and teachers are unknown to each other and the unknown is unpredictable and often threatening.

The fear of changing is similar to many teachers' fears of their students. Change is not controllable or predictable and though it is possible to provide teachers with hints on how to open up their classroom the main burden is on them.

I have found that the best way to proceed is to identify one specific thing that I am afraid to do with my students but that would make our lives together more comfortable. This may involve doing simple things like touching one's students or letting them call you by your first name. It might mean leaving the classroom unsupervised for a few minutes every day and allowing the students to become able to get along with each other without the presence of an adult.

Fear of the loss of one's job is real, though less so if one has tenure. However, there are risks to be taken. I found myself in the position of having to decide whether I would maintain my job or my self-respect a number of times during my teaching career. And I have lost jobs. However, there are many things one can do to effect change that involve smaller risks. Every individual must face the problem of the value and honesty of his or her life's work at some time.

*I can't change because the parents won't understand.* Educating parents to accept change in the schools is not an easy matter. However, parents do respond to teachers who know their children as individuals, and who express obvious concerns for their children's interests and future lives. It is always more convincing to parents if changes in their own children are used as illustrations of what open learning is all about rather than citations from books by experts or abstract discussions about freedom and authority.

There are some parents who will never be convinced that an open classroom makes sense for their children. They should be provided with the option of transferring their children to another class in the school. Teachers always trade off a number of students anyway, so why shouldn't this tradition be used to allow parents the choice of the classroom most suited to their and their children's needs.

During the first year of change it is difficult for teachers to convince parents of the value of their work because they are groping themselves. It is much easier the second year. In fact, the greater confidence the teacher has in his work the easier it is to convince parents of the value of the work for their children.

*I can't change because open learning will harm my students in their future schooling.* I have not found this to be true. Students who function autonomously in open classrooms can, if they choose, adjust to many circumstances. They know what to expect from different teachers and can change their styles. Further, students themselves are increasingly taking the initiative in changing their schools to meet their needs and often it is next year's teacher who needs to worry about survival, not the students.

*I can't change because the time isn't ripe.* There isn't much I can say about this excuse. If the time isn't ripe to change now, then it might be in a few years, if there are any schools left. Jim Herndon, author of *The Way It's Spozed to Be*, once said at a teacher's meeting, "The only reason people don't change is because they don't want to." Jim did not mean that changing was an easy thing. It is difficult to face one's life and rethink it, to change comfortable or at least workable modes of behavior. Yet my feeling is that now for many of us we can do no less than rethink our lives and act for our own as well as our students' survival.

If the times were not ripe for change in 1971 and 1972, think about 1981 and 1982. Times do not change things, people do. There are many positive reasons to overcome one's excuses and participate in trying once again to build creative classrooms and caring schools. Here are five:

1. *Self-respect.*   The self-respect of teachers comes from the tone and quality of their work in the classroom. When you care about your work, are close to your students, and when you all enjoy spending time together learning, there is no finer, more personally rewarding work in the world. Nor is there any way to develop respect other than through the quality of life people share with each other.

2. *Personal growth.*   A person cannot grow if he or she follows directions mechanically and acts against his or her own beliefs and judgment. Teaching well and teaching poorly are both hard work. Being with large numbers of children five or more hours a day is not easy. However, if teaching leads to growth, to entertaining new ideas, and developing new skills for both teacher and student, then the energy put into the work

leads to personal enrichment and makes it possible to sustain a life of teaching. Teaching poorly and with resentment shrivels the soul.

3. *The power that comes from having a control over your work.*

Risking change, acting on your beliefs and ideas leads to empowerment. Students are not the only ones who benefit from learning how to make choices and initiate programs. A great deal of the fun and satisfaction of teaching comes from those aspects of the work that teachers plan and control themselves.

4. *The pleasure of helping young people grow.*   I believe the essential characteristic of excellent teaching is the desire to see one's pupils grow. The phenomenon of growth is the substance of education and when growth is stifled or distorted, teachers are as damaged as their students. One simply has to fight to be allowed to develop an environment that encourages growth or give up on the possibility of teaching well.

5. *The obligation we have as citizens to encourage democracy.*   Public schools were created to provide opportunities for successful adult life to all the children of all the people in our society. Public school teachers have a disproportionate burden of trying to make democracy work in our society. As hard as that task is, it is what lends dignity and value to our work and we must remember that, no matter what attitudes towards public education are current.

I hope the material in this book will add substance to the work of teachers who continue to care about children and teaching and refuse to be intimidated by pressure that has no regard for the empowerment of children.

# 1
# Reading
# and Talking

# A
# Comprehension
# and Conversation

On the significant themes that can lead to interesting conversation in the classroom and the
desire to read, including detailed consideration
of how to teach reading.

*T*he keys to reading and writing well are speech and comprehension. The ability to speak well and thoughtfully, to weigh and evaluate the meaning of a text, and to deal with ideas and feelings in writing are the basic components of literacy. Phonic skills, spelling and grammar, and "correct" pronunciation are secondary skills which can easily be mastered if reading and writing are understood as significant human activities. It is easy to forget that though these mechanical aspects of literacy may be necessary they are not sufficient to develop the skills of reading and writing. The ability to spell or punctuate or read words with the correct pronunciation is not equivalent to the understanding of what you read, just as the ability to produce grammatic sentences is not equivalent to writing well.

We are now facing what could be called a crisis of comprehension in most of our schools. The mechanics of phonics, grammar, spelling are not the central problems our students face. Their main problem is that they have not learned to understand or speak intelligently about what they read, or to write coherently and intelligently about what they think. Major causes of this functional illiteracy are the impoverishment of the content of what is read, the elimination of open-ended discussion and conversation in the classroom, and the obsession with mechanics at the cost of meaning. It is essential to reestablish a sensible relation between comprehension and expression on the one hand and mechanics on the other.

One of the most dramatic illustrations of the crisis of comprehension occurred at a school I visited several years ago. I had just attended a reading conference, and a colleague and I got into a discussion about the relationship between phonics skills and reading comprehension. Joan told me that several years ago the staff at her school decided they had to do something about the increasing number of students there who had severe reading problems. They adopted a new program that strongly emphasized phonics.

After a few years of hard work, almost all of the students had acquired phonics skills and were now testing at or above grade level on the phonics part of standardized reading tests. However, with that success a new problem surfaced: the comprehension scores of the students had actually dropped. The staff is now facing the curious problem of having students who can sound out words but who don't understand what they're reading.

Since Joan's school isn't too far from my home, I suggested that I spend a day observing. That day I noticed some aspects of the reading program that provided clues about why the children were having trouble with comprehension. First, the students seemed rushed. As soon as they caught on to one skill they were moved on to another work sheet. There seemed to be no time for them to practice and use what they had learned, much less savor it. Generally, they appeared to be reading books in order to acquire phonics skills rather to be moved or amused or to learn something new. Moreover, when they did do exercises for comprehension, all they had to do was answer closed-ended questions in simple declarative sentences. I particularly remember one question and one student's answer: "Do you think John liked to go shopping with his uncle?" "I do think that John liked to go shopping with his uncle."

The student's response was as machinelike as the question. Though the answer was correct, it was nothing but a transposition of the words in the question, requiring no exercise of thought, imagination, or analysis.

I mentioned my perceptions to Joan. She acknowledged that even though she had felt that the phonics program had positive aspects, she had also felt pressure to rush the students from skill to skill in order to meet production quotas set for her by the program's teachers' manual. She had had little time to read aloud to her students or talk with them in a casual way about what they had read. She said that she was beginning to feel more like a systems manager and file clerk than a teacher.

I suggested that Joan set aside a half hour a day to work with reading, listening, and talking in a different way, one that would emphasize content and comprehension. During this half hour, she would abandon the individualized reading activities and work with the whole class. Moreover, since analysis, thought, and understanding are preceded by interest, all the activities they would do together would be based on challenging and important themes in the lives of her students.

During my years of teaching I've identified a number of themes that I believe are interesting to almost all children. Some of them are: having the power of adults; running away from home; finding someone to express one's innermost thoughts to; feeling rejected; experiencing death; experiencing requited and unrequited love; having a secret club that functions independently of adults; overcoming some weakness or handicap; being poor or homeless; having secret powers over things and people; understanding and experiencing fairness and unfairness; and learning one's cultural identity.

Joan decided to choose two or three themes and find some children's books that deal with them. Then, during that half hour she planned to set aside for listening and talking, she would read from those books and talk with the class about the significance of their themes.

What seems most important to me is dealing with the themes rather than merely the simple facts of the story. The development of comprehension comes from learning how to question a text, how to discover its main themes, and how to evaluate the way in which it deals with those themes. There are also times when studying a theme itself and finding books that illustrate it can be the central activity in your language curriculum.

There are many ways to go about using significant themes in the context of reading and writing programs. Here are elaborations on how to use some of these themes which engage students' minds because they involve issues that arise for any growing person:

## 1. Fairness and Unfairness

One of the most provocative questions I've asked children is, "Have you ever been treated unfairly? "Everyone seems to have a list of examples and in the course of giving students a chance to express their perceptions of what is unfair it makes sense to list the basic kinds of abuses they experience. For example, a shorthand list might look like this:

> not allowed to eat what I want,
> not allowed to stay up,
> made to wear clothes I don't like,
> made to do chores,
> not treated as well as brother,
> picked on by some adults.

After reading the list over with the class it is possible to generalize a bit. Unfairness sometimes consists in being prevented from doing things one wants to do; at other times it consists in being made to do what one resists. A third instance of unfairness consists in being treated less well than other people. All three forms of perceived unfair treatment lend themselves to writing and discussion and are embodied in many interesting books on almost all reading levels. For example, the following themes can be used for writing or story telling:

Write or tell a story about a world in which no one could do anything they wanted to.

Write or tell a story about a world in which you were always made to do what you didn't want to do.

Write or tell a story or monologue from the point of view of a person who is being treated unfairly.

Write or tell a story or monologue from the point of view of someone who is treating others unfairly.

Write an essay telling about what a world in which everyone was treated fairly would be like, or have a class discussion on the rules and behavior that would exist in a fair world.

Some books that could be read and discussed in the context of dealing with this theme are: George Orwell's *Animal Farm*, which deals with the development of a society of unequals; Judy Blume's *Blubber*, in which a young person is treated unfairly because she's fat; R. R. Knudson's *Zanballes*, in which girls are treated unfairly because of stereotyped views of what is appropriate in girls' sports; and Alex Haley's *Roots*, in which the subjects of racism and the resistance to such unfair treatment are central. These books help take the issue away from particular instances of unfair behavior and lead to more general considerations of fairness and justice. Though these books are not easy to read, well-chosen excerpts can be read aloud or used as reading texts. There are times when a particular scene or dramatic incident is accessible to young children when the whole work would be too complex and inaccessible.

### 2. Learning Who One Is— Cultural Identity

Alex Haley's *Roots* is an obvious source to use when discussing people's search for their origins though there are many other sources ranging all the way from the very simple *Are You My Mother* to complex novels like William Faulkner's *Absalom, Absalom* (which means "my son, my son") and James Joyce's *Ulysses*. It is possible to weave bits from complex novels, simple story books, photographs of family reunions, and old people's reminiscences into a discussion of where students' families came from and what life was like *for them* in their places of origin. One way to begin is to ask children to find out where their grandparents came from and then, as they tell the class, put a pin on a map of the world indicating that place. It also helps to start things off yourself and describe your own grandparents. I find students fascinated by the fact that one set of my grandparents came from Poland and another from England. In the course of discussing my origins with a number of different classes I've gathered different resources: the record and script of *Fiddler on the Roof* which provides a romanticized version of life in Polish-Russia in the early 1900s; a super-8 print of Charlie Chaplin's *The Immigrant*, which shows people coming to America in steerage; a collection of Marc Chagall's prints full of Jewish-Polish-Russian cultural symbols; and a copy of *Image Before My Eyes* (by Lucjan Dobroszycki and Barbara Kirshenblatt-Gimblett, Schocken Books) which contains photos of the often not pleasant reality of my grandparents' birthplaces. Using this material plus a prayer book my grandfather brought with him from Poland, I share my cultural and geographic roots with young people and at the same time give them hints about the kind of material to gather about their own roots.

After getting a map of class origins done it's possible to group students together for further exploration and writing about their origins. In the course of doing this I've seen students make many fascinating discoveries. For instance in one class three students discovered that they all had some Cherokee blood though one's family came from North Carolina, another's from Oklahoma, and a third from Stockton, California. I asked the students to try to find out why the Cherokee came from these places and in the course of their explorations the students came upon and wrote movingly about the trail of tears and the dust bowl years and how it personally affected them.

Some of the best resources to use in class explorations of roots are writings done by previous students about their roots. In fact it probably makes sense to integrate the exploration of cultural roots into the curriculum every year and give students an opportunity to come back to the question of their roots continually with greater depth and a wider range of resources.

There are mythic origins as well as historic ones and the study of myth can also provide a basis for discussion, writing, and the development of comprehension. I remember once reading a class a Seneca Indian "origin" tale: "A man who was a Crow was traveling. He didn't know where he had come from or which way he was going. As he moved along he kept thinking: 'How did I come to be alive? Where did I come from? Where am I going?' "

One student responded immediately, "You know, I've had the same questions. Did the Seneca Indians worry about those things too?"

I used this unexpected response to talk about the concern that people, from as early as we can trace, have always had about their origins and their futures. "Where did I come from?" "How did I get to be the way I am?"

These questions seem to be as old as language. Every mythology begins with accounts of origins—how the earth came to be, why there is order instead of chaos, how people were created, why people walk upright, how language was made, how food and shelter originated. Here, for example, is an Eskimo tale of origins:

"There was once a girl who lived in the open desert of white snow. One day she went in a boat with a man who suddenly threw her into the sea. When she tried to hold on to the side of the boat, he cut her fingers off so that the boat would not turn over. She sank to the bottom of the sea where she made her home inside a large bubble. Here she became the mother of all life in the sea. The fingers she had lost grew into seals and walrus. And the people of this frozen land now had food to eat. Now they had skins for warmth. Now they had oil for the long nights of winter."

In this tale the mother of all life in the sea is a person who has been harmed. But the fingers she lost became food for people. The destructive can become creative. This simple story embodies a way of looking at people and their relationship to nature—a unity of life to be respected.

Mythic figures aren't only from the past. The lives of many contemporary characters encountered on TV and in the theater also represent versions of how things began and why they are as they are. For many young people, the most powerful mythic figures created in our time are those found in comic books. The stories of the origins of comic book superheros reveal aspects of our culture just as the Eskimo myth displayed some values of that culture.

In discussing and reading about origins, students are fascinated when some of the contemporary superheros they know so well from comic books and TV are included. Take Superman for example. He is an alien born on the planet Krypton, which was destroyed in an atomic holocaust. He was saved by his parents and sent to Earth. He is stronger and purer than the rest of us. The alien Superman becomes our hero and protector. He presents human frailties only through Clark Kent, his earthly identity. The savior of Metropolis, a mythic city, is not one of us. Is the message that we can't save ourselves?

Wonder Woman has an equally interesting origin. Born on Paradise Isle where no man lives, her original name was Princess Diana. During the Second World War, Steve Trevor, an American pilot, crashed on Paradise Isle. He and Princess Diana fell in love. Eventually she had to choose between love and loyalty to the Amazons, her people. One of the early Wonder Woman comics describes her choice: "And so, Princess Diana, the Wonder Woman, giving up her heritage and her right to eternal life, leaves Paradise Isle to take the man she loves back to America—the land she learns to love and protect, and adopts as her own!"

Again an alien comes to rescue us. This time her motive is love. For Superman the motive was to prevent Earth from destroying itself the way Krypton did.

The Hulk is a more recent superhero. The story of his origin is the reverse of that of Wonder Woman and Superman. The Hulk was born a human, Bruce Banner, who became a famous nuclear physicist. In experimenting with physical forces beyond his control, Dr. Banner found himself transformed into the Hulk, a physically superhuman though subintelligent force. Bruce Banner and the Hulk are a contemporary version of Dr. Jekyll and Mr. Hyde. It is never clear, however, whether the Hulk is a positive or a negative force. The problem posed by the Hulk is whether science is positive or negative when it gets the upper hand.

Mythology is open ended. We can all create our own villains and superheroes. One way to get your students involved in writing is to have them create their own characters and make their own stories or comic books. Students' first efforts will usually be direct imitations of the comics they have seen on TV. However, thinking about the origins of their creations can help students clarify and develop them. The tales of their beginnings can be a springboard for stories that don't depend on stereotypes drawn from comics and TV. Where did these new mythic figures come from? How did they get their powers? Do they have relatives? Are there limits to their powers? Do they need to eat or rest or be fueled? Do they have any connections with their old lives? All these questions help create in-depth characters and give a reality to the imaginary lives created by your students.

Young people enjoy making up wild explanations for things whenever they have the chance. Here are a few examples of origins themes that can lead to interesting writing:

1. "Why are . . .?" tales. Why are owls creatures of the night? Why are there stars? Why are there so many animals? Why are there night and day? Why does it rain?
2. "Why is there . . .?" tales. Why is there hair? Why is there love? Hate? Laughter? Tears?
3. "Why do . . .?" tales. Why do people live in the air and fish live in the water? Why do animals let themselves be tamed by people? Why do people stop growing? Why do living things die?
4. "Why don't . . .?" stories. Why don't animals talk? Why don't people fly? Why don't trees walk? Why don't stones cry?

Considering our own origins, those of superheroes, and even the everyday things that are often taken for granted has appealed to my students no matter what their age. It gets them thinking, reasoning, imagining, and writing.

### 3. Overcoming Weaknesses or Handicaps

The word "retarded" is often used carelessly and cruelly by young people. They call each other retarded and even call things that don't work well or break easily retarded. A while back one of my students referred to his brother's retarded car which was always breaking down. He also called a few of the other students retarded. When I asked why he used the word *retarded* so much he said it just meant dumb and stupid, like deaf and dumb. Then I pressed a bit and asked if deaf also meant dumb and he said yes. At that point it was important to discuss the whole question of handicaps so I asked my students to imagine themselves born deaf. Then I asked them to try to communicate with each other without saying a word. In order to make the task more complex I had the students get in pairs and gave one student in each pair a message to convey to the other member of the pair. The messages read:

Let's go bike riding tomorrow.
Did you do your homework yesterday?
What did you have for dinner last night?
My father will come to visit me next month.

Trying to communicate was very frustrating for the students, and after a while we discussed how hard it is to create your own language, and how difficult it must be for deaf children and their hearing parents. We also talked about the fact that deafness has no relationship to retardation, and began to clarify the meaning of "retarded." In the course of our discussion I read sections from *In This Sign* and *Deaf Like Me,* which deal in dignified ways with the world of the deaf. I also shared Remy Charlip, Mary Beth, and George Ancona's (*Parents Magazine* president) *Handtalk: An ABC of Finger Spelling and Sign Language*, and Lewis Fant, Jr.'s *Sign Language* (Joyce Media Co., Box 458, Northridge, CA 91328) with the class, and after a while a number of students used sign language with each other regularly.

After considering deafness, we talked about the tragedy of actual biological retardation. A recently published children's book, *Welcome*

*Home, Jellybean* by Marlene Fanta Shyer, deals with a retarded girl whose mother decides to remove her from a horrible institution and integrate her into the family. The book is full of scenes that show the frustration retarded people have to live with, and the problems they inadvertently cause for other people. The book also manages to make the retarded girl seem attractive and courageous, and provides a strong counterargument to any cruel and thoughtless ways of thinking about retardation.

There are many other things that can be done with the theme of overcoming weaknesses and handicaps. There are books and films like *The Other Side of the Mountain, The Autobiography of Helen Keller,* and *The Door in the Wall* that deal with overcoming handicaps. There are others like *The Hunchback of Notre Dame, Of Mice and Men, The Phantom of the Opera,* and *The Elephant Man* that deal with the problems of having a deformity or handicap. This can lead to discussions of why some human characteristics are found repugnant and others attractive. In this context it also would be possible to discuss how taste is culture bound; how, for example, in some cultures a hunchback is considered magical and a source of good luck while in others it is considered evil.

Finally it is possible to extend the concept of overcoming a handicap to include group responses to disasters like floods and hurricanes. It would be possible, for example, to discover some local disaster (in San Francisco the earthquake would be a logical choice) and by reading and talking to people, study a particular community's response to a natural disaster.

### 4. Requited and Unrequited Love

"Does Dick love Sally? Does Sally love Dick?" I once posed these questions playfully to a group of second graders and found myself engaged in a serious discussion about affection. The students considered all the possibilities:

> Dick loves Sally. Sally loves Dick.
> Dick loves Sally. Sally doesn't love Dick
> Dick doesn't love Sally. Sally loves Dick.
> Dick doesn't love Sally. Sally doesn't love Dick.

After a while I suggested that some students act out the different situations, and then introduced the notion of unrequited love and of requited love.

Unrequited love ranges all the way from loving John Travolta and knowing he'll never love you, to complex personal triangles of the sort Jean Paul Sartre describes in *No Exit*, where one person loves a second person who loves a third who loves the first.

Probably everyone has experienced unrequited love in one form or another and has stories to tell and write that involve one or another of the Dick and Sally variations.

There are many ways to introduce the exploration of the nature of love and, by extension, romance. Karen Hubert in her excellent book *Teaching and Writing Popular Fiction: Horror Adventure Mystery and Romance in the American Classroom* (available from Teachers and Writers Collaborative, 84 Fifth Ave., NY 10011, $4.00) has dozens of suggestions on how to discuss and write about romance and love. Here are just some of her twelve pages of suggestions: Start by asking the class "Where and how do lovers meet?" Ask the class to make a list of places and circumstances. "How do people feel when they first meet each other? Do they necessarily like each other right off? Write the thoughts of a person who meets someone but doesn't like him. Does her first impression change or stay the same by the end of the first date or first evening together? What is a first impression? Write one. Remember, the main sensation in a first impression is newness, strangeness."

The topics of requited and unrequited love provides a wonderful opportunity to introduce children to some of the classic stories of litera-ture, to stories like Romeo and Juliet, Tristan and Isolde, Anna Karenina, Don Giovanni, La Traviata, and Rigoletto. It's possible to read or play excerpts from these works, but it is also possible to simply tell the story to your class and discuss it. I remember using the printed scenario and illustrations of Rigoletto while telling a sixth-grade class the story of Rigoletto. I paraphrased the story and showed pictures of certain scenes. Two or three times I paused and played an aria from the opera. I wasn't sure how the class would take this but their minds were involved in the jealousy, love, and revenge of the plots. As long as they knew what was happening in the story they could feel their way through the musical excerpts I played.

The themes of requited and unrequited love and the other themes mentioned here, tie together reading, writing, talking, thinking, and feeling. Often the most surprising result of teaching through the themes, to content, is that students read and write on levels beyond their mechanical skills, and that learning takes place in leaps and bounds rather than at a slow steady pace. It takes time and experience to develop the confidence to center one's teaching on content and use instruction in skills as a supplement. However, it makes life in the classroom more interesting and learning more personal and therefore more meaningful to the student.

### 5. Power

The theme of power is crucial throughout life. Every sane person wants to be powerful, but everyone accepts the idea that there are limits to human power. The wish to overcome these limits gives rise to dreams and tales of secret and special powers. Such dreams and tales have a special place in children's imaginations because children are doubly powerless. They have the same limits as adults as well as those related to not being fully developed. Myths, fantastic tales, and comics provide rich "secret power" material for use in the classroom.

One way to take advantage of such material is to use it to help children invent and develop characters for themselves that can fit into a collective story. I first realized the effectiveness of this technique (and the intrigue of the "secret power" theme) a few summers ago when, during a family vacation, my children asked me to make up a story for them. I thought it would be fun to make a story that included them and that they could participate in. First, I dreamed up three characters who paralleled my children in age and sex. "Mimi" had the powers of a crab. She could live in and out of the water, had powerful hands that could turn into superpincers, and had a hard, shell-like skin. "Tutu" could climb anywhere, and whenever she wanted she could grow powerful horns that shot fire. "Jha" could live under the earth and had a powerful poisonous stinger that he kept in his back pocket. Because he could get in between cracks in a wall he was a very good spy.

I chose these characteristics because my daughter Tonia's Zodiac sign is Cancer (the crab), Erica's is Capricorn (the goat), and my son Josh's is Scorpio (the scorpion).

I added a final character called "Overall" who occasionally came to rescue the children or set them out on a new adventure. He was made of formless smoke, could take any form he chose, and spoke with a Bronx accent.

Each night I would begin a different adventure. For example: "One day Mimi wandered off to the seashore. She felt like being alone that night. The reason was . . ." Then I turned to Tonia and she gave the reason. Taking up on her hints I followed the direction she gave the story and brought the other children and their characters in as it progressed. If one of the children had nothing to say, I just went on myself. It was great fun to do this with my own children, and it gave them the chance to think their way through situations and problems. So I decided to try a similar storytelling technique with the "secret power" theme in the classroom. Now I've used it in second-, fourth-, and sixth-grade classrooms, varying the material for the different grade levels.

I began by introducing the theme of secret powers. Consciously trying to keep my students out of the rut of concentrating on the usual comic book superheroes, I started with Greek mythology. We read and told tales of the battles of the Titans and of the Trojan Wars and of the jealousies and struggles among the gods. I explained that the gods had special areas they controlled, and special powers. Ares, the god of war, had power to stir things up, but, he was dependent upon Hephaestos, who made the weapons. Poseidon controlled the sea and its creatures. No god had all the power and each one could act only according to his or her nature.

I was fortunate enough to have the tapes and books of *Heroes, Gods and Monsters from the Greek Myths* (Spoken Arts, 310 North Ave., New Rochelle, NY 10801), which has a marvelous collection of oral and visual materials. This enabled the students to listen and, when they were able, read the tales over and over again. They discovered such weapons as the shield of Diana, the staff of Hermes and the trident of Poseidon, and such creatures as the Sirens, the Cyclops, and the Hydra. Already their repertory of possible powers, weapons, and ideas were enlarged beyond the realm of comic books.

Next I played tapes of old radio shows to the children. We discussed the origins of the Lone Ranger and the power of invisibility of the Shadow and even did a few radio shows using the class cassette recorder. (The Shadow, The Lone Ranger, and hundreds of other old radio shows are available on 33⅓ lp recordings from Murray Hill Records, One Park Ave., New York, NY 10016.)

Finally we got to comic books and discussed the Fantastic Four, Spiderman, Wonder Woman, and a few others. Since the students had already been exposed to myths and other forms of "super" and "secret" powers, they were able to compare different forms of stories using such characters. I made a list of things the children could focus on as each worked to develop a character for himself or herself for our collective story.

*1. Character Traits.*   To avoid creating shallow heroes, I suggested that students think about such qualities as courage, humor, intelligence, and feelings. The fantasy game *Dungeons and Dragons* (TSR Hobbies, Inc., POB 756, Lake Geneva, WI 53147) directs each player to create a personality for his or her part in the game. Each character is rated on the following traits: strength, intelligence, wisdom, constitution, dexterity, and charisma. A toss of a die determines whether the character is strong or weak on each trait.

I decided to have my students concentrate on courage, strength, sensitivity, health, luck, trickiness, honesty, and intelligence in developing their characters. Instead of using a die, I set up the rule that each character could have two very strong, three medium, and three weak traits. The students would choose their own combinations. Thus, one student chose trickiness and strength as strong traits while another chose intelligence and luck.

*2. Name.*   As we began to talk about character traits it became clear that names were needed to help focus the activity. Students can choose names in a number of ways: from astrological signs, from versions of comic book superheroes, from such traits as strength ("Strono," "Strength Woman," and so forth), from Greek mythical names recombined ("Appolonia," "Cyclops II"), from animals ("Python," "Elephant Boy"), from parts of the body ("The Fist," "Fang"), and so forth.

*3. Superpowers and Flaws.*   I explained to the children that heroes who have no weaknesses are boring because they always win, and you always know that they are going to win beforehand. There is no excitement in a story unless the heroes have special secret weaknesses as well as secret strengths. One student pointed out that Superman's weakness was Kryptonite, and another that Wonder Woman lost her powers if her lasso and bracelets were taken away. To add a bit of historical perspective I added Achilles' heel to the list of classic flaws.

We agreed to give each character one major flaw. One student suggested that we write down the flaws and let only the storyteller know them. Then everyone would have to guess each others' flaws. In one class we tried it that way, and in the other two all the students knew each others' weaknesses.

It took quite a while for us to get through these first three dimensions of creating a character. We talked about traits and strengths, and because we would all be involved in common stories, all the students had to know about each others' character sketches.

After several weeks each student wrote a description of his or her character. I duplicated enough copies of the descriptions so that every student could have one of each.

*4. Costumes and Weapons.*   Each student was allowed to pick a special weapon. One of the superheroes, "Combinative Man," had the power to control people's minds and souls. His weapon was a shiny buckle that could capture the sun. He took over people's minds when he shined it in their faces. Another hero, who had Medusa's power to turn people to stone, chose a hammer and chisel with which she could carve stone people into the forms of others before returning them to life.

This character used a special everyday mask to conceal her true identity. Many of the other heroes had everyday clothes for the same purpose, then wore costumes when they were playing the hero's role. Some of the costumes were quite elaborate, and the children drew detailed pictures of them. Other costumes were sketched roughly or merely described in words. A few of the students wanted their heroes just to wear everyday clothes all the time.

*5. Origins.*    By this time the students were anxious to get on with the group story. I suggested that at the same time anyone who wished to could work on a story about the origins of his or her hero. A few students chose this option and later told their stories to all of us.

## Setting and Action

In order to prepare myself to help the children invent a group story, I planned certain aspects in advance. This can be done with the students if you think they'd be interested.

*6. Setting.*    First I considered the *time* factor. Should the story take place in the distant past—perhaps prehistoric times, when the dinosaurs roamed the earth? Or should it be in the future—including all the fantastic scientific and technological dreams and nightmares it might hold? Or should the story start in the present? Once the time factor was decided, we had to determine the place. Should the story take place on earth or on another planet? In a familiar or a strange environment?

I chose to place our story in the present, in a small town in a remote mountainous area where Bigfoot and other such creatures were rumored to exist. This gave us a settlement of ordinary humans and the possibility of adventure in the wild. Once a location in time and space is chosen, most of the context for the story is set.

One further helpful bit of advance planning is establishment of the cultural environment of the story. Is it set in a working-class community or in a wealthy suburb? Are the people Black, Asian, White, Chicano, or mixed? Is there the possibility of unusual beings—ghosts and dragons—or are the students' characters to be the only ones who have secret powers?

Once you decide on a locale, there is just one more thing to plan.

7. *Enemies.*   What will be the story's conflict or problem? Will there be some specific supernatural superenemy, such as a terror or monster come to haunt the place, or a human enemy? Or will the enemy be something like a flood, fire, or storm?

I chose an enemy suggested to me by a San Francisco teacher who heard me talk about these ideas. She suggested that smog and monsters who are born in, live in, and eat the smog, might be the enemy. My smog monsters were immune to all forms of destruction, and the only way to get rid of them was to get rid of the smog. In order to accommodate this plot to my locale, I put a lumber mill and a refinery in my town and had the mountains covered with a mysterious reddish-brown haze from which horrible shrieks and screams emanated on moonless midnights.

Before I began the first story I described the locale and then asked a student to describe her hero. Then I started: "One day Cheetah [that was her hero's name] was driving along in her sports car. She came to a little town called Drain, California. There was not one person on the streets. All the stores had thick black shades that were closed. The only thing moving was smoke coming out of the chimneys of some big brick buildings on the edge of town. So Cheetah got out of the car and she . . ."

I turned the story over to the girl for awhile. When she told about Cheetah getting out of the car, looking around, and finally deciding to go into a restaurant, I interrupted, and we had a conversation about the horrible noise and the fear that gripped the town. Then I said, "Cheetah figured that this was a problem she could solve, but that she needed the help of three other people who had secret powers since she couldn't tell whether her powers were useful." Three other students volunteered. In finishing the story, they battled the monsters of the smog to the end. Then I started another story involving four other students.

I felt this approach to developing a theme worked well because it got my students talking and thinking about character traits and gave them an opportunity to listen and talk to each other—not just to me—and it was fun. As a final activity, I suggested that students involved in developing the same stories work together to write them. The finished products have become a permanent part of their class libraries.

## 6. Transformations
## and Voyages or Adventures

One theme that has been on my mind for as long as I can remember and that I recently shared with my students is voyaging into unknown worlds. Perhaps it's because my grandparents who migrated from Poland to the United States in 1906 used to tell me about the shock and confusion they experienced when they found themselves in a new and very different world. Or maybe it was my own realization as a child that it was possible to be mobile and change rather than accept the world you are born into as inevitable. However, my thoughts about mobility and exploration were vague and unfocused until the sixth grade when, quite by accident, I discovered Howard Pease's book *The Tattooed Man*. I had found one of my voyages and, fascinated, I read the book in one night.

*The Tattooed Man* is about a young man's sea voyage to search for his brother, who had been accused of jumping ship and making off with the company's money. As I read the book, I could imagine myself at sea trying to make sense out of the complicated and mysterious life aboard Tod Moran's ship. There were so many exciting elements. Tod's parents were dead, and he was on his own. He was free to go where he chose and make decisions for himself. In fact, he was everything I felt I wasn't but wanted to be.

As I reread the book recently and relived those early dreams and aspirations, I was more and more eager to share them with my fourth, fifth, and sixth graders. First, I read the children some selections from *The Tattooed Man*. Though the language was a bit old-fashioned and some of the ideas socially naive, the theme of being on one's own, engaged in a voyage of exploration and adventure, was as exciting to these youngsters as it had been to me as a child. We decided to explore various journeys of adventure and see if we could create our own.

### On Our Way

Many of the students had seen the movies *The Golden Voyage of Sinbad* and *The Seventh Voyage of Sinbad*. They loved the magic and the animation of monsters in the films. One student said that he was really frightened by the "homunculus," a creature made of dirt, blood, hair, and nail clippings, that was created by an evil magician in one of the films. Through secret spells known only to him, the magician put his own soul and energy into the little batlike creature. The magician grew older and weaker as the creature came to life.

Picking up on the fascinating theme of putting one's energy into the creation of another creature, I suggested that the students imagine transformations of their own. One girl imagined concentrating all of her energy into calling forth a blue two-inch-tall miniature horse that could fly. Another student imagined turning into steam and mist, floating from place to place, and then materializing suddenly as himself and frightening people.

We discussed transformations for a few days, and some students imagined voyages they took with these creations as their companions. We didn't write down any of the adventures. I wanted the children to let their imaginations go and not feel that they had to commit themselves in print before they had a chance to really explore the theme.

I am coming to realize more and more the value of discussion and storytelling as a preliminary to writing. Students are willing to let their imaginations fly when they don't have to worry about completing a sentence or getting on with a paragraph. They are more willing to invent, to sketch, to play with language. The play gives them ways of working out and eliminating many possibilities before deciding on a theme that they are willing to work out on paper to share with others.

### Arrival at Our Destination

After about a week of taking turns telling each other tales of voyaging adventures, I summarized what I thought were the main themes we had come up with and listed them on the chalkboard:

> imagining that you have no parents or close relatives and
>     have to make your way in the world;
> voyaging to find a lost or kidnapped relative;
> going on a quest to recover stolen treasure;
> having a mythical creature come to you, ask for help, and go
>     with you on an adventure;
> running away from home;
> being stranded in a strange place with a person who does not
>     speak the same language and having to figure out a way to
>     communicate and survive.

Next I suggested that the students pick one of these themes and, using their favorite characters from those they had made up the week before, write a tale of mystery, adventure, and travel. The students are working on these stories now. And I'm working to develop these themes into a more thorough unit on imaginary voyages with another group of students next year.

To research the subject, I've been looking at some of the classic literary voyages to see if they can provide starting points for discussion and writing. So far I've found a number of rich resources and have confirmed my feeling that the subject of imaginary voyages lends itself to an integrated reading, writing, and discussion program that could certainly last several months.

*Don Quixote.*   This wonderful book can be the source of a number of interesting themes for writing: the foolish quest, the search for the impossible, the voyage of self-deception, and the idea of having a companion on one's voyages. Sancho Panza, as well as being a delightful character, provides a model for the sidekick—Tonto to the Lone Ranger, Robin to Batman, Kato to the Green Hornet. Some students will want to create imaginary companions to help them move their stories along and rescue them from difficult situations.

*Gulliver's Travels.*   Here is the prototype of voyages to strange worlds. The main character doesn't change but is thrown into a world where everything is different from everyday reality, so he or she is required to make adjustments. Another aspect of Gulliver-like voyages is that the main character is seen as strange by the inhabitants of the world he or she visits. A lot of science fiction depends on this kind of device, which is summed up by the title of Robert A. Heinlein's popular science fiction novel *Stranger in a Strange Land*. I've found that young people immediately get the idea and are fascinated by it.

*Odyssey.*   The voyage home is a rich theme for writing. All that's necessary is to set up a situation in which someone is lost and has to overcome obstacles while trying to find the way home. I recently read a Horatio Alger book called *Adrift in New York* about a boy who was kidnapped and living with people who pretended to be his parents even though he knew they weren't. This is one version of the theme. Another could begin with characters waking up after a long sleep, finding themselves in an unfamiliar world, and having to overcome all sorts of obstacles while finding their way home. Reading or telling the story of the *Odyssey* is a good way to introduce this theme.

*Pilgrim's Progress.*   On voyages of growth and salvation, the characters grow up, learn something new, gain greater command of their worlds, understand more about the nature of reality. It may be difficult for some young people to get the point of a voyage of salvation. I'm thinking about introducing the idea by making up my own story about a young boy and girl who don't feel good about themselves and who are faced, quite accidentally, with a challenge that they overcome. Through this incident they learn that they are strong and needn't worry so much about themselves.

I find that I quite often have to make up such stories on the spot in order to explain some complicated idea to youngsters. The stories don't have to be very good. They just have to make the point. Children's imaginations are so rich that the simplest story can become a vehicle for them to create interesting characters and express deep feelings. I have noticed that sometimes all I have to say is something like, "Once there was a girl named Susan whose dog got run over by a car" and the children have already filled in their own details and are open to hearing anything about what Susan did.

*Orpheus.*   Tales of voyages with the threat of defeat at one wrong move are really tales of temptation and distraction. Orpheus goes to Hades to rescue Euridice and is told that if he turns around to look back he will lose her forever. Stories of this sort can be based on simple temptations like offers of candy or money. Or the issues can be more serious through bargains for friendship or power. Before asking students to write tales of temptation, I think it is important to talk a lot about what tempts people, what gets them to avoid doing what they know they should do or makes them do what they know they shouldn't do. Again, discussion is a key to providing the groundwork for interesting writing.

There is much more research that could be done to develop the theme of imaginary voyages. There's Dante, Jules Verne, the Bible with the stories of Moses and Ruth and the Wandering Jew, the tale of Darwin's discoveries on the Voyage of the Beagle and other tales of geographic exploration and scientific discovery. However, one has to stop using resources at some point and let the students begin to use their own imaginations. With this as with all the other significant themes one has to balance classical and historical material with contemporary tales and with the products of young people's imagination. This balance is central to the development of a rich and interesting language program.

# B
# *But Where's the Reading Program?*

On how to develop an integrated reading program that combines phonics, reading, test-taking skills, talking, language games, and writing.

*W*hen I was teaching first grade most visitors to the classroom seemed puzzled about the nature of our reading program and often leapt to the conclusion that there was none. They might have arrived in the middle of a discussion of power or fairness, or seen a play involving the students' superheroes. Or they might have arrived when I was reading with one student and the rest of the students were busy with their own play or projects. They wanted to see a reading program and couldn't find it in the complexity of the activity that went on in our room.

In most schools, reading programs are defined in physical as well as educational terms. There is a box of reading materials, an area designated as the reading center, a time set aside as "the" time for reading. The program is usually developmental and has a long list of developmental skills prescribed for each student.

There was nothing of the sort in my classroom, and yet I had a coherent and comprehensive reading program. What I describe may at first seem a bit random, but with some patience I think it is possible to see how all the pieces fit together.

In one corner of the room sits a book-making table. On it are rubber stamps—of the alphabet as well as such characters as tigers and sea horses and clowns and hearts. There is also a variety of crayons, felt-tip markers, pencils and pens, pastels and water colors plus a number of empty, stapled together books, lots of paper and a stapler. On a shelf near the table are about 50 books in progress.

Nearby is another table covered with commercially produced books—some picture books, copies of *Hop on Pop* and other standard, easy-reading books as well as the few basal texts the district has provided us with—and a few of the books written and illustrated by the students. There is also a chess set on the table and an illustrated book on how to play the game.

Across the room is a place to explore in math and science. A small electronic calculator, lots of poker chips, math workbooks and work sheets, Cuisenaire rods, and some simple books on arithmetic are out for the students to use. Near that are science materials—perhaps there are bells and batteries and bulbs. The objects vary from one time of year to another. Some simple science books written by the students describing what can be done with the equipment are also available.

There is an art table as well, with paints and clay and pencils and a whole series of how-to-draw books. I have discovered these do not inhibit the children's creativity and often stretch their skills beyond what one could imagine.

On the walls are poems and short stories and books and illustrations, almost all of which are the work of the students. The impression on walking into the room is that paper and writing instruments are the basic materials of our curriculum.

In the middle of the room, there is a large rug where the children can play with blocks and a haunted house where they can pursue their fantasies in private.

I usually station myself at one of the tables in the middle of the room with my box of key-words. The key-word box contains words the students have chosen to learn—one a day.

Not every student uses the box, but each day I ask a number of the children to give me a word they want to learn, write it for them and ask them to write it down and illustrate it. After a month, of course, the word-a-day generates twenty words.

One of our kindergartners who seemed to avoid reading completely, loved to ask for a word each day and at the end of two weeks knew "violet," "witch," "mama," "pork chop," "ice cream," "rat," "fist," "Herb," "yes," "no" and then wrote the following story: "I am a violet witch. My mama loves ice cream."

### Assessment

During the first hour-and-a-half of the day, the students can work at any tables they care to, build with blocks or play in the haunted house. There is, however, one catch. During that time they will be asked to read to me. We sit together and talk about what is being read. I try to help the children learn to describe and analyze what they are reading. During that time I can also assess what the student knows and needs to work on. I find that spending five minutes a day, a minimum of three times a week with each child is all that is really needed to get young people reading and to solve their problems as readers.

### Playing, Working, Learning

In addition to these short individual reading times, I occasionally give a five-minute, group lesson that deals with using words in interesting ways. One lesson, for example, is on compound words. I write the following words on the board:

```
hot                                                    dog
                        air plane
in                                                     side
                   up    town
```

Then I ask the students to help each other read them. After the students figure out the words, I start scrambling them:

```
hot    plane
air    dog
up     dog
in     plane
hot    town
```

We play with the words while reading them. Instead of telling the students it was time to learn compound words, they learned by playing with language. To me that seems to be one of the keys to teaching reading, to create experiences in which language is explored and played with, rather than to turn creative and funny experiences into drill.

After a break outside in the yard, we have some group work. The students either work on Cuisenaire rods, write their own books or illustrate a story I have written on the board. During the course of the year, I expect students to become increasingly independent.

### Story Writing

At the beginning of the year, I ask and often insist that at some time during the day, the children sit down and make up and write a story. Half-way through the year options develop—students can work on their own books, make up their own stories, create comic books. I get looser as the year goes on.

Usually a writing lesson begins with my asking, "Who wants to tell a story?" Sometimes one person tells the whole story; at other times, it is a collective effort.

Recently three students working together developed this story:

> *Once there was a porcupine. It felt ugly and ran away from home. A kid ran after it and told it he loved its points. So it came home.*

After the students write the story, I ask them to read it back to me and illustrate it.

Sometimes I have a "dookie" problem with these stories. The problem is a common one. "Dookie" is the current word the class uses for feces. One of the students loves to turn every story into a "dookie" story and is always the first to volunteer when I ask who wants to do the story.

It is a question of how one deals with censorship on the first-grade level. For example, one day last week, he promised to tell a "straight" story, and this emerged:

> *Once there was a kid who built a rocket ship. It went to the moon. It almost crashed but got there safe. It landed. The crew got out and stepped on the moon and saw dookie.*

The children in the class loved the story, and I was afraid that I would be stuck in "dookie" for months. My decision, which the students seemed to accept without much protest, was that we could do one "dookie" story a week. I gave as much as I could, and they accepted "dookie" as one part of the world—not all of it.

(While this solution works for me, it may not be realistic for all teachers in all situations. Know your community—both in school and out—before you establish your own policy. It is also advisable to prepare school administrators and concerned families. If you inform both groups of your purpose beforehand, angry parents will not be complaining to startled administrators about the work their children bring home and the "terrible things" that go on in your classroom.)

## Test Skills

Through these experiences with language, students learn to read and enjoy it. Their focus is on the magic of words and not on exercise and drill. Nevertheless the class is provided with a solid well-thought-out reading and writing program.

I often get asked if I teach basic skills and, of course I do but not in a rigid way. At the beginning of one school year, I decided to take the initiative and announced to the other teachers at the school that I intended to put a heavy emphasis on basic skills that year. One co-worker said he was glad to see that I had finally come around and realized that children need structure in order to learn and that traditional drill and basal readers weren't bad after all.

There was no time to respond, and the conversation ended on an awkward note, since the children were arriving and we both had to be back in our classrooms. Like most things in school, there simply was no time to explore the issues and see them through to a resolution.

However, I have been thinking a lot about what we said to each other. It is important to keep two things straight—what you want to achieve and how you intend to get there. Much of the debate over basic skills confuses these things. The other teacher and I agreed on goals. We both believed that our students should learn to read and write and be competent in arithmetic. Because we agreed on this, he assumed that we must also agree on methods and educational philosophy.

Goals do not imply methods nor do they lock one into a single philosophy. I do not see the need to use basal readers and believe that drill and the teaching of the rules of usage can be confusing and can actually interfere with learning. I also believe that learning does not occur through the mastery of small developmentally sequenced skills in a step-by-step way, but rather occurs through insight and understanding with different skills and bits of information falling into place. This occurs in different ways for different people, and much of what is taught in developmental programs is acquired through this process.

For me the process of learning to read in a classroom should be continuous with the informal ways in which children are exposed to print all around them even before they come to school. Children in our society are surrounded by words. When they get up in the morning, they wash with a bar of soap that has a brand name inscribed on it; they brush their teeth with toothpaste that announces its manufacturer. At breakfast their parents drink a certain brand of coffee; they eat a favorite type of cereal. Just this morning my children had a mixture of Cheerios, Grape-Nut Flakes, and Raisin Bran, and my four-year-old knows which cereal comes in which box. With all its cans and boxes and packages and bottles, the kitchen is a veritable reading lab. The same is true for TV and, in urban settings, the street, rife with billboards, signs, and graffiti.

Children are exposed to an enormous amount of print outside of school and play an active role themselves in trying to figure it out. They develop fairly large sight vocabularies and manage to pick up a smattering of phonics (coffee and candy start with "c", men's and milk start with an "m" sound). One of the problems children face in school is that this exposure, as well as their personal efforts to understand print, has little or no relationship to what is called "learning to read." Many reading programs assume that children bring nothing with them to school.

From my perspective one of the main roles of teachers is to understand what their students know outside of school and to connect this knowledge and experience with what goes on in the classroom. School should be an extension of the rest of one's life and not an instrument of alienation. The classroom can be set up and the reading program designed so that students can draw on their own experiences and take advantage of strengths already developed.

First, teachers must know something about their students' lives. One way is to spend some mornings together, having breakfast at the homes of several of your students and then accompanying them to school. For some teachers an afternoon and evening is better. In either case, the point is for you to note all the words and forms of writing they encounter in the course of a day.

If your schedule does not allow for such a plan, you will have to rely upon an imaginative reconstruction to the lives of your students as well as upon what they tell you about what they see and do, of the foods they eat and the other products they consume. The least you can do, however, is to take a "word walk" around the school neighborhood and the students' neighborhood as well, if the two are not the same. Copy down all the words you encounter and compare your lists.

From this information you can begin to design a print environment in which the students feel knowledgeable and strong. On a primary school level, it is sensible to start with the most easily recognized and familiar words—labels and boxes and cans and street signs. Coca Cola, Wheaties, Sanka, and Cafe Bustelo might all be part of that early sight vocabulary, depending on the community you work in.

In my kindergarten/first-grade class, I covered a bulletin board with boxes and packages and labels and made one of our first reading activities Read-A-Box Time. We looked at the boxes, read the labels, talked about the contents and their health value. Nutrition, the development of oral language, as well as sight vocabulary and a knowledge of the sounds of initial consonants, went hand in hand and started from words that were familiar to the students.

I also made up a set of flash cards using all the product names. On one card was a label from a box or a can. On another card, I wrote the word from the label. Many of the students could identify Coca Cola when written in the form found on the bottle but couldn't recognize it when simply printed.

One of the games the students played was matching a word printed on a label with the same word written out. This was done to help the students become flexible in understanding the variety of print faces and be able to read words as words and not solely as pictures. There were a number of other games we played with the cards, ranging from simple read-a-card games to making up stories with the cards and developing shopping lists and estimating how much it costs to buy a bag of groceries. The room was also filled with signs, such as Beware of Dog,

Apartment for Rent, Trespassers Will Be Eaten, Open, Closed, Stop, Exit, Dead End and one of the students' favorites—No Eating, No Swimming, No Bikes, No Pets, No Picnicking Allowed. If nothing else, all the children quickly learned how to read and spell "no" after looking at the sign a few times. The sign itself led to several interesting discussions of why things were prohibited, what sensible prohibitions were and why people sometimes said no just for the sake of it. Again, reading, life outside of school, talking, and phonic skills were integrated.

For older children and often for the younger ones as well, there is a wealth of material one can use—car ads, menus, bus schedules, newspaper ads, handbills, comic books, airline schedules, travel brochures, signs and ads from local stores, price tags, loan agreements, lease forms, tax forms, ADC and food-stamp applications, food stamps, bills, parking tickets, stereo ads, mail order catalogues, programs and scorecards from sports events, local newspapers, concert posters and tickets, record handouts promoting the latest rock or soul or gospel group. Reading at any age connects with life outside of school.

This doesn't mean that all one does in a reading program is use popular culture. Reading can assist young people in moving beyond the immediate into exploring otherwise inaccessible aspects of human experience. A wide assortment of books of all types and on all levels of complexity, including basal readers, is in our classroom, and students can choose to use them or not. *Hooked on Books* by Daniel Fader and Elton McNeil (Berkeley Publishing Corp.) describes many ways in which paperbacks can be used in the classroom.

Just as a variety of books can be used rather than a single reader, student writing can go far beyond work-sheet drill. Writing is an act of inner exploration, a discovery of one's own voice and a process of finding out and saying just what one believes and thinks. I try to have my students do a piece of writing each day—a story, a thought, a small poem, or a description—something in their own voice so that they will learn to write easily as they learn to read.

For some students a bit of judicious and well-selected drill or phonics is called for. My principle is to use no more drill or formal teaching of phonics than is absolutely essential for an individual child. Sometimes someone will stumble over a sound or not understand a particular aspect of reading (for example, the way "th" sounds at the beginning of a word or the way "ou" functions). Then it is up to the teacher to explain the principle involved and to give the student an opportunity to practice that skill.

Work sheets can be useful, and I especially like to make them up on the spot to meet specific needs. They should not, however, be used to fill up the time in a school day and keep children busy and quiet. I fall into the trap every once in a while and shove a workbook in front of a student who seems restless and about to get out of hand. Now at times like that, I use other activities that involve the child and do not attach a negative association to learning, such as suggesting that a student work on a jigsaw puzzle, write a story, make up a comic book, play a game.

The hardest thing for teachers who begin to use informal reading materials, books, and student writing as the substance of their reading program is that it will not be possible to measure where every child is at every moment in traditional terms. The way to get around this is to set up your program so that you will be able to sit and read with each child at least once a week. Even though you won't know which color workbook they are in or at which level on the behaviorial objective scale they fall, you will know a much more important thing—how well they are reading.

There is one common objection to this informal approach to reading. Knowing how to read does not necessarily mean a child will do well on reading tests that evaluate specific skills knowledge and the ability to follow directions. And there is currently no way of escaping the powerful effect test results have upon young people's educational opportunities. For this reason, I find it necessary at certain times to prepare my students for dealing with the standard devices used to sort people.

After my students have learned to read with some ease and confidence, I introduce them to the kind of questions they will be expected to answer on the standardized tests, such as:

> What is the main idea?
> What is the best title?
> What sounds like —?

I try to make it clear that being able to deal with tests is a special type of reading and not at all like being able to write a story or read someone else's story or read a book. And I try to make it as clear as I can to five- and six-year olds that tests do not judge character or intellectual ability but only the ability to conform to certain, easily learnable ways of functioning.

Our students learn how to read and how to take tests, too. It is my hope, however, that a time will come when the pleasures that can be derived from knowing how to read will be valued in and of themselves by students and teachers everywhere, and that our current obsession with testing will be remembered as a strange obsolete custom.

# C
# *Play With Words: Spelling and Vocabulary Revisited*

A creative approach to spelling which shows how to integrate the study of word origins, word play, and the expansion of vocabulary into a spelling program.

*T*he ability of children to read and write is judged according to their ability to read and write the words that make up basal readers and phonics workbooks. I have been struck by the number and range of words that young people are able to recognize and reproduce in writing that never appear in textbooks or are considered part of their working knowledge of written languages. So-called obscene words embody a range of vocabulary, not all four-lettered, that most students whatever their academic status master easily and without being taught in school. However, one does not have to look at the forbidden or socially "improper" to find an even greater range of words that supposedly nonliterate children can read and write. The category of names provides an almost inexhaustible list of words they master outside of the classroom.

Once I asked several fifth- and sixth-grade teachers whose students were "functionally illiterate" to ask their students to make lists of all the names they knew. The results were astonishing—several lists were three and four pages long and the shortest of them contained more than 15 names. Here's a sample list:

| | | |
|---|---|---|
| Alice | Johnny | Philip |
| Babs | Gloria | Nelly |
| Bobby | Junior | Nikolas |
| Thomas | Judy | Sava |
| Henry | Grace | Al |

Not all of the names were spelled correctly but the students' guesses were often phonically correct. Moreover the students did the assignment as if it were the most natural thing in the world. Many youngsters who wouldn't touch any other written assignment made the list of names with ease and enthusiasm.

This shouldn't have surprised us, though it did. Names are magical signs bound up with the identities of their bearers. To know someone's name is to have power over him—to be able to call him forth and dismiss him, and talk about him. Many Black kids feel that teacher's don't know their names. The rejection this implies is often cause for student defiance.

Children love to play with names, twist them and distort them, turn them into nicknames (nicked-names) many of which are harmless but some of which really hurt. The old rhyme:

*Sticks and stones may break my bones*
*But names will never harm me*

is only partially true. In the Black dialect of English to "call someone's name" is to mock their name, and the act of calling someone's name (especially someone's mother's name) can lead to a serious fight.

Teachers are not immune to having their names mocked and twisted by their pupils. Nicknames for teachers are common. More interesting, however, is the way students use teachers' proper names. Teachers must be addressed as Mr. ———, Miss ——— and Mrs. ———. Their first names are not used by their pupils, perhaps because their use implies familiarity and therefore takes away from the power of the teacher. Students love to discover their teachers' first names and use them at unexpected moments. I have seen teachers outraged when addressed familiarly and have seen students punished severely for such acts. To know a teacher's first name is to know that she is human. This is a source of power for young people and a threat to teachers insecure about their roles as authorities.

Students do not only know lists of names of their friends. They also know product names. (Ajax, Marlboro, Salem—how many cigarette brand names do you think the most illiterate sixth-grader could reproduce?) They know names of movie stars and recording stars and sports heroes and television personalities. Many boys who are supposed to be unable to write can reproduce the full names of the last three heavyweight boxing champions. There are few young people who cannot spell James Brown or Ray Charles or Muhammad Ali or whoever the latest hero happens to be.

The names of popular songs are quickly learned by students, especially those who own records and want to be sure that they are not stolen or that the record they put on the phonograph is the one they told their friends was coming on. I have known students who cannot (or perhaps will not) read "Dick and Jane" or even the *Bank Street Readers* who nonetheless can read the titles of songs such as "Freedom," "Walk on By," "Say it Loud," "Two Lovers," "Chain of Fools," "The Duke of Earl, "Natural Woman" . . . Many students can even reproduce the words of these songs.

Individual names are not the only names young people know. There are group names: Temptations, Supremes, Animals, Beatles, Oakland Raiders, New York Yankees, Tigers, Pirates, Jets, Mets. . . .

There are lists and lists of names that young people are familiar with. One can easily discover many of these names. Look at the inside covers of notebooks, at the covers of textbooks, on casts, on the tops of desks, on the walls of the schools and the neighborhood. Yet all of this knowledge of language is generally useless in school. Often teachers do not even bother to inquire into the names their students know or the culture implied by the knowledge of those names. It is worth finding out and the easiest way to find out is to ask. It is surprising how open children are to displaying what they truly know and care about to adults who are interested. Finding out how many names one knows and can reproduce can be a delightful game, and can lead one toward an understanding of the complexity of our culture and the unsuspected grasp of language that supposedly nonliterate members of our society have.

Playing with lists of names can also be an interesting experience for teachers. List all of the team names or personal names or product names you know. Ask other people to do the same thing. Read the lists. It is astonishing how we are all bathed in words, and how verbal our environment has become. An awareness of the degree to which we are surrounded by letters and words on television and billboards and window displays can lead to making the classroom itself a rich verbal environment full of words interesting to look at and related to the culture of the young people who inhabit our classrooms.

Of course, this is just a beginning. There are many exciting words students haven't yet encountered and many words they use carelessly that can be used in more interesting ways. Spelling, a superficially mechanical exercise, can be turned into a wonderful study of word origins, meaning, and play and invention with language.

At one point in my teaching I grew tired of hearing my own children and my students complain about spelling lessons. I would have liked to simply stop teaching the subject and hope that the students would acquire spelling ability by reading a lot and absorbing the principles informally. I know that many of them do learn spelling that way,but I also know that some don't. Moreover I hoped then, and believe now, that spelling can be a vehicle for extending young students' understanding of language and for introducing them to the romance of words. I decided to accept the challenge of making spelling interesting rather than abandoning it, and I think that to some degree I've succeeded.

One of my most successful techniques for enlivening spelling has to do with those words that students often confuse. I refer to words that are close in spelling and meaning like *accept* and *except, credible* and *credit-able, boiled* and *broiled, peasant* and *pheasant*. I found that if I took words that were confused with each other and put them together in a meaningful sentence, I provided my students with a device that helped them sort out the meanings and spellings. Thus, sentences like "He boiled an egg while the deer he caught broiled over the fire", "I would like to accept your invitation except that I've already been invited to another party", and "The peasant caught a pheasant" seem to help students understand nuances of meaning. This is a skill that is certainly essential to the development of complex reading ability and a sophisticated writing vocabulary.

At about the time I began introducing my students to pairs of similar words, I discovered *Room's Dictionary of Confusibles* (Routledge & Kegan Paul). The dictionary contains approximately 100 pages of sets of words that can be confused with each other. Using the book and the help of a number of friends who remembered confusibles that had puzzled them, I developed several lists of confusibles that I have since used for spelling lessons.

Confusibles and several other word groupings have helped me broaden the meaning of spelling lessons to include understanding nuances of word meanings and something of the history of words. Through these lessons I've found it possible to engage my students in discussions about the nature of language and about the problems they have in grasping the complexity of English. In fact, in each lesson a third to a half of the words are given to the class by students themselves. There is no reason why students cannot be involved in curriculum planning.

Here are three lists of confusibles on three levels of complexity. I pieced these together with the help of students, friends and *Room's Dictionary*.

### Level I Confusibles

1. *fiend/friend/find*
2. *solid/stolid/staid/sedate* (In this case the spelling is quite simple, but the comparison of meanings is complex.)
3. *warp/weft/woof* (This led to a discussion of weaving and of words that stand for animal sounds like *woof, bow wow, moo, meow*.)
4. *dazed/dazzled* (The students found the distinction between these words fascinating. One boy came up with this sentence that we all agreed was a fine way to clarify the distinction: "He was dazed because she dazzled him." Someone suggested we consider the in-

verse: "He was dazzled because she dazed him." One girl said the sentence meant that he was impressed because she could upset him so much. This was a good example of a discussion that dealt with the nuances of language in a way that was meaningful for the students.)

5. *afflicted/inflicted* (My students' favorite sentence for these words was "He was afflicted by the stab she inflicted.")

### Level II Confusibles

1. *assure/insure/ensure*
2. *compound/confound/confuse*
3. *progeny/prodigy/protégé* (One sentence we came up with: "One of my progeny is a prodigy and a protégé of Muhammad Ali.")
4. *benevolent/beneficent*
5. *pendant/pedant/pennant*

### Level III Confusibles

1. *acid/acrid/acerbic*
2. *aggravate/exacerbate/exasperate*
3. *frantic/phrenetic/fanatic/frenetic*
4. *abdicate/abrogate/arrogate/derogate* (See if you can come up with a sentence for this one.)

## People Phrases

Confusibles are not the only way to infuse spelling with some spirit and make it a thoughtful, perhaps enjoyable activity. A group of phrases in our language (no reason why a spelling list should consist of words alone) that derive from the lives of certain individuals arise from interesting stories and intrigue students. Many of these phrases are listed and described in *Whose What?* by Dorothy Blumberg (Holt, Rinehart). Here are some that I've used for my spelling list:

**1.** *Achilles' Heel.*   A person's particular weak spot. Some of the Achilles' heels that students have claimed are a weakness for people who offer them candy, a desire to please people they know they don't like, and an inability to say no even when they don't want to go somewhere.

**2.** *Mrs. O'Leary's Cow.*   The cow that supposedly started the great Chicago fire. Considered as a metaphor, the cow is something small and insignificant that causes a major event, like a simple remark that sets off gossip and causes people grief.

**3.** *King Solomon's Ring.*     A magic ring worn by Solomon, which gave him the power to understand the speech of birds and animals and power over living and spiritual creatures. This spelling phrase led to discussions about magical powers and objects that can convey them. It is a good phrase to use as a starter for writing about special powers.

**4.** *Diogenes' Lantern.*     The lantern the Greek philosopher Diogenes used walking about the streets of Athens looking for an honest man; metaphorically anything that will reveal a deep truth, perhaps one that cannot be uncovered. Diogenes implied in his work that there never was an honest man.

**5.** *Robin Hood's Barn.*     This English phrase probably referred to all of Sherwood Forest. An English saying states that someone who is led on a wild-goose chase has been "all around Robin Hood's barn."

### Origins

A third category of spelling words are words that have interesting origins. These words have stories that can accompany the spelling list so that spelling and reading can be combined. Here is a small sampling of words with stories. You can find hundreds of these in *Thereby Hangs a Tale* by Charles Earle Funk (Warner Paperback Library) and in other paperbacks that Funk has written.

*1. Disaster.*     This literally means "against the stars." A disaster is something that occurred because something displeased the higher powers.

*2. Trophy.*     A *tropaion* was a figure constructed by the Greeks on a battlefield out of the arms, legs, weapons and uniforms of enemy soldiers. If the enemy allowed the Greeks to construct a *tropaion*, that was a sign that they were in retreat and that the Greeks had won. It didn't take long for someone in the class to comment that the figure on our athletic trophies should not be those of the winners but rather those of the losers, who have been taken over by the winners.

*3. Escape.* "Es" means out of and "cape" means just what it does today, a cape one wears. To escape is to throw down your cape and get away fast. It also came from the idea that if someone grabbed your cape and you could untie it you could leave them holding the cape.

*4. Science.* This word comes from the same root as scimitar, the curved sword of the Turks. The root means to cut through, and science, in the original sense, meant to cut through to the truth.

### Body Spelling

A final group of spelling phrases can be developed from a cluster of ways of using parts of the body. Taking the hand for example, it's easy to develop a list including: *handsome, handy, a bird in the hand is worth two in the bush, hand-to-hand combat, hand-to-hand living, hands off, hands down, hand picked, hand out, hand-me-down, and so forth.* The cluster of words can be used for spelling and for discussions of how an object becomes an image and expands the power of our language. A good source for clusters like these is *A Dictionary of American Idioms* edited by Maxine Boetner and John E. Gater (Barron's Educational Series).

For a final list, here are some heartfelt words: *Hearty, heartless, heart-to-heart talk, heart warming, eat one's heart out, cross one's heart, from the bottom of one's heart, lose heart,* and, as one of my students added, to have had spelling words to *one's heart's content*.

Recently I have been working with Cynthia Brown and with the artists Kirby Leary and Steve Oliff to turn this play with words into spelling workbooks. Shown on pages 47 to 56 are two sample lessons from our books which are available for $2.50 each from Continuity Press, 40561 Eureka Hill Rd., Point Arena, CA 95468.

One can also go beyond single words or simple phrases and play with images in the classroom. Consider for example this statement: "Stop bugging me you ape. You have to be loony or cuckoo. You look asinine pulling that hoggish monkey business. Do you expect me to lionize you for your waspish and dogged behavior? I'm not that gullible you cocky, crabby weasel. You won't be able to worm your way out of this one. I may seem like a lamb, but when you try to skunk me you have to realize that you have a tiger by the tail."

Though it is unlikely that anyone would actually talk this way, our everyday language is full of images drawn from animal life. Looking at such images can provide young people with insights into the creative

# Shades of Meaning

Things come in all sizes. There are many words to describe whether something is big or small. Here are some:

## ① minuscule

Something is minuscule if it is so small you can hardly see it. A speck of dust is minuscule.

## tiny ②

A gnat is tiny. It is very small. The word tiny is sometimes used to compare things. A very small giant is a tiny giant, and a very small mouse is a tiny mouse.

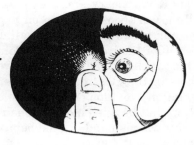

**³ small ⁴ medium ⁵ large**

Small, medium, and large are used to compare sizes. In this picture the elephant is large, the bear is medium, and the boy is small.

**6 HUGE**

An ocean liner makes people seem tiny. It is huge.

**7 ENORMOUS!**

Enormous makes huge seem small. The enormous giant is surprised at how small the ocean liner is.

## 8 VAST...

The ocean is vast. The Sahara Desert is vast. Something incredibly huge, but still able to be measured, is vast.

## 9 INFINITE... ∞

Something that goes on and on without end is infinite. There is no end to space and no highest number. Both are infinite.

## ·Exercises·

**①**

a. Imagine that you are the size of a flea. What would it feel like to be living on a dog?_____

_____

_____

_____

_____

b. Now imagine you are an enormous giant. What does it feel like to see all the tiny creatures around you? _____

_____

_____

_____

_____

**②** Make a list of the smallest and the largest things you have ever seen:

|         -smallest-          |          - largest -          |
| --------------------------- | ----------------------------- |
| a._____          | a._____            |
| b._____          | b._____            |
| c._____          | c._____            |
| d._____          | d._____            |
| e._____          | e._____            |

③     Sometimes the way you write shows the meaning of the words you write. For example: tiny is tiny, and **LARGE** is large. Using this space, try to show differences in size by the way you write the words in this lesson.

Look at the words in this lesson for a few minutes. Now try to write them all down from memory.

_____     _____
_____     _____
_____     _____
_____

If you didn't succeed, turn back and try again.

_____     _____
_____     _____
_____     _____
_____

Fill in the words that you missed.

# Lesson 2: Words with Stories

## 1. jack-in-the-box

In England 300 years ago the word "jack" meant something that was worthless like junk or rags. Some tricksters would persuade people that boxes full of jack had gold and jewels in them and sell the boxes for real money. Now a jack-in-the-box has a monster or a clown in it. It still contains a surprise.

## 2. a blue moon

A blue moon happens when two full moons come out in one month. This happens about once every 150 years, so the phrase "once in a blue moon" means almost never.

## 3. freelance

Freelancers are people who work for themselves. A free lance was a soldier whose lance or spear belonged to no one but himself. He was a soldier for hire, someone who would fight on the side of anyone who paid him. The word goes back 400 years when there were many freelancers wandering about Europe. Another word for a freelancer is a mercenary.

## 4. bonfire

Bonfire used to be spelled bone-fire. Thousands of years ago in the middle of summer, people in England would gather up all the bones of animals caught and eaten during the year. They would pile up the bones and set a big bone fire. No one knows why they did this.

## 5. hoodwink

To hoodwink someone means to fool them. The word comes from the time when people wore hoods and cloaks. The word "wink" meant to blind someone. Thieves used to pull people's hoods over their faces and blind them when they were escaping. Now the word means to fool or trick someone in a clever way.

## 6. chow

Chow is food. Chow dogs were raised in China for food. Make your own conclusions about the origin of this word and think of them when you find yourself in the chowline at lunchtime.

## 7. figurehead

A figurehead is someone who has a fancy title and no power. Sailing ships used to have curved figures at the front of their prows. These figures were beautiful but made of wood.

## 8. an old chestnut

An old chestnut is a boring joke or story you have heard too many times. People think the phrase comes from the play "The Broken Sword" where this conversation takes place:

Captain: I entered the woods when suddenly from the thick boughs of a cork tree...
Pablo: A chestnut, Captain, a chestnut.
Captain: Bah, I tell you it was a cork tree.
Pablo: A chestnut. I guess I ought to know, for haven't I heard this story 27 times?

# Exercises:

1. Write in your own words a definition of the spelling words and phrases:

jack-in-the-box _____

a blue moon _____

freelance _____

bonfire _____

hoodwink _____

chow _____

figurehead _____

an old chestnut _____

2. Write a sentence using the words & phrases:

| jack-in-the-box | _____ |
| a blue moon | _____ |
| freelance | _____ |
| bonfire | _____ |
| hoodwink | _____ |
| chow | _____ |
| figurehead | _____ |
| an old chestnut | _____ |

3. Draw a line from each word or phrase to its closest meaning:

jack-in-the-box      — one who has a fancy title but no power
a blue moon      — to fool or trick someone
freelance      — a box containing a surprise
bonfire      — a boring joke
hoodwink      — almost never
chow      — people who work for themselves
figurehead      — a fire of bones
an old chestnut      — food

4. Look at the list of words and phrases on this page. Now cover them and try to write them down from memory:

_____  _____
_____  _____
_____  _____

If you didn't succeed, cover them and try again:

_____  _____
_____  _____
_____  _____

Fill in the words you missed.

use of language. When I wrote this paragraph on the board in a third-grade class, the students were delighted and enchanted. They found the language, which to me was full of clichés, fresh and exciting.

All my students used the expression "bugging" but not one of them had ever thought of it in terms of a bug crawling under their clothes and bothering them when they just couldn't catch it. After we discussed the phrase, one student said "some people are really like that—they get under your skin." Someone interrupted and said, "people don't really get under your skin, it's just that they make you feel that way."

### The Magic of Images

At that point I introduced the notion of an image. Part of the magic of language is that we can use images from all our experience and knowledge of the world to express our feelings and thoughts in a condensed and yet accurate form. Language has the magical quality of fusing images to create exciting, meaningful statements. Images are not unique to poetry or literature. They are the substance of our everyday language.

I began to try to explain these ideas to the class, but some students were getting impatient. They wanted me to get on with the animals. In particular, they wanted to know how the word "gullible" relates to a sea gull. I asked what gulls eat, and someone replied that they will eat anything. At that point some of the students laughed with understanding. They knew immediately, without a dictionary, exactly what it meant to be gullible.

Then I asked everyone to write down all the words or terms they could think of that come from animals' lives or characteristics and are used to describe people or actions. Here is a partial list: dirty dog, eats like a pig, works like a horse, be chicken, to goose, eagle eye, big as a whale, busy as a bee, ponytail, mousy, wolf your food, catty, stud, fleeced, stool pigeon, birdbrained, old bat, clam up, to parrot someone, henpecked, foxy, cool cat, old hen, stubborn as a mule, a ball hawk, a shrimp, batty, eager beaver, and puppy love.

I duplicated our list, and a few days later we examined these images, talking about what a particular animal led people to choose it to represent a human characteristic. Then I suggested that the students make up their own images using objects, colors, living things, machines, anything they wished. Here are a few of the images they developed: looks like a flat tire, is a sharp scissor, is a bus stop, is a centimeter not an inch, robot eye, smiles like a dentist, is an empty soda can, is a Cheerio, stencils his words, Cadillac eye.

I encouraged the children to work their own images into their writing and to watch for images in what they read. It made sense to talk about images before talking about similes and metaphors and to start with spoken language before getting to poetry and written language. I wanted my students to see for themselves that all language is full of imagery and that we constantly use comparisons and contrasts to convey ideas and feelings.

### Learning from Other Creatures

I wanted to show something else, too, something I feel we forget because we are so surrounded with objects of our own manufacture. I wanted the children to realize that we not only borrow images from nature but also learn from other creatures and owe them the respect we owe our best teachers.

To convey this idea in a less abstract way, I asked the class to think about spiders—what people may have learned from them and how this knowledge may have affected language and thought. That initial question was not concrete enough either, so I had to rephrase it. I asked the class to think of things spiders did that reminded the students of things people do. One child said spiders catch their food; another added that spiders build their own houses and a third said that in order to do that they weave a web. That was the answer I was after.

Usually my questions are more open ended. I want to follow the flow of the students' thoughts and ideas. Occasionally, however, I like the children to follow my thinking because I am excited by an idea or have done a lot of research and want to share what I have learned.

This time I was motivated by an article, "What a Linguistic Contexualist Thinks of Philosophers," on English words that were taken from weaving. (The article, by Edwin Herbert Lewis, was published in the Summer, 1976, edition of *Outlook*, an educational journal put out by the Mountainview Center for Environmental Education at the University of Colorado at Boulder.) Weaving is a central image for much of our thinking. Words such as *text* from *textile, alignment, accordion, background, bag, chord, fiber, edge* from *edging, know, knit, lace, lash, line, pack, slack* and *bias* all come from weaving. Think of the many uses, not connected with weaving or sewing, of words like *bias* and *line* and *text*. One particular word derived from weaving surprised me—*order*. The word was originally a technical term that meant to begin a web and by extension to lay a warp on a loom.

As I explained this to the class, one student asked me if people learned to weave from spiders. My response was that no one knows. Weaving seems to be such an old form that there are only mythical tales about the origin of the craft. However, the images of weaving and building spiderwebs have been connected for a long time, and the language of weaving and the language describing a spiderweb are very close.

Certainly the spider is one of the symbols of the weaver—the creator of order out of randomness or chaos, the builder of fabric out of unorganized strands. Thus, the animal and the human craft similar to the work of the animal are used as images for a central idea in all of our lives—that of bringing things together, of weaving a coherent fabric out of our lives and developing some organic order for ourselves and our community. In traditional tales spiders are respected for their wisdom and pesistence and are models for people.

For many of the students, our talk about images made language seem flexible and changing, creative and open ended for the first time. If people could look at the world and make images to describe their experiences in the past, it could still be done. New images and words could be made, and old ones could be given new meanings.

One girl seemed quite troubled, though, by what I had said. She asked how a person could ever tell that the word *order* or other words originally came from somewhere else and were images. She even showed me that her dictionary didn't say anything about where the word *order* came from.

## More on Language Origins

I thought about going on to explain to the children that the substance of the work of many poets and writers is to remake language so that it becomes appropriate to new ways of experiencing. Instead I did something much more concrete at this point in our study. The next day I brought in several etymoligical dictionaries of the English language. (I think *Origins* by Eric Partridge, Macmillan, is the best.) I suggested that by using these dictionaries that tell about the origins of word meanings, we make our own dictionaries, discovering one interesting word origin a day.

I also proposed that a section of our class dictionary be left open for new words created by members of the class. These dictionaries are a good substitute for vocabulary and spelling lists. In fact, they have become vocabulary and spelling lists that are generated by the children.

# II
# Approaches
# to Writing

# A
# Planning and Managing
# a Writing Program

A system for planning and managing a writing
program that allows students and teachers to set
writing goals and evaluate progress in an on-
going way.

*A* recent experience I had working on developing writing programs points up how much managing curriculum areas in the classroom can vary. In trying to decide how we could best help our students with their writing, the teachers I was working with and I got into considering class-management systems in some depth. We saw that a classroom in which space, time and life are planned for a whole school year and which seems well organized is often quite static and unresponsive to changes in student needs. It isn't necessarily beneficial that classroom procedures or relationships among students be the same on the last day of school as they were on the first.

On the other hand we realized that a system of management that accommodates changing student needs can, in reality, be just as well organized *and* more effective. This more dynamic system begins with a certain structure and, over the course of a school year, is modified systematically to achieve specific educational goals. A school subject can change and at the same time be managed in a controlled way from September to June.

Writing is one subject that particularly lends itself to dynamc management since students gradually change their writing and work habits as they become more skilled in, and comfortable with, exploring a variety of written forms. Therefore, to develop our writing programs, my colleagues and I focused on the changes we wanted to be able to accommodate as our students' writing evolved over the course of a school year.

### Setting Up a Structure

To begin, we made a chart with three headings: "Where We Came From," "Where We Are" and "Where We Are Going." The "Where We Came From" section listed students' previous writing experiences. These included details for such aspects of writing as speaking, grouping, grading and correcting, developing ideas, revising and selecting a style and voice.

The "Where We Are" section gave starting points for a writing program, taking into account the nature of students' previous experiences in school. We gave such careful attention to their prior educational background because we didn't want to overwhelm them with too many choices and materials. Each of us in the group had had the experience of underestimating the negative effects of drill-oriented learning. We had seen such techniques paralyze students, blocking original thinking and questioning.

Our chart's third column, "Where We Are Going," articulated the goals we established for an effective and creative writing program. As one teacher mentioned, the chart itself could be used as a program description and as an outline for lesson plans as well.

### Speaking and Writing

Speaking was the first aspect of a writing program we considered. We agreed that most of our students were accustomed to the speech mode politely called answering. The teacher or the textbook asks a question and the student answers. We agreed that many students had never had the opportunity to spin a tale or carry on an open-ended conversation in class. Our chart showed that we had acknowledged that passivity. We decided that we would try to add a bit of the unexpected to our program.

The "Where We Are Going" student goals we developed were for students to be able to freely tell stories, compose poems on the spot, play with language and read their own works to each other. We thought a good starting point would be for students to do dramatic readings from plays, to read newspaper stories aloud as if they were radio newscasters and to select a favorite passage from a book and read it to the class after practicing with a friend. All of these semistructured activities are transitional and only part of the dynamic program we would be managing. They give students an opportunity to express themselves and yet don't require them to create the content. After these transitional stages, we would have to plan steps and phases that would encourage students to speak more freely and interestingly in the classroom.

### Grouping

The next aspect we listed was group size for writing exercises. If our students had had any experience in writing in class at all, most of them had been given, as a whole group, one specific topic to write about. Our ultimate goal was to have a variety of writing projects going on at the same time, to have small groups writing together, to have individual novels and poems at various stages of development and to have occasional group discussions about the progress of our writing.

Choice is the key to making the transition here. We decided to begin by giving whole-class assignments—but with choices. We also felt that from the beginning we should give our students the opportunity to pursue individual projects instead of writing with the group. Through our dynamic management we would eventually eliminate the whole-class writing lessons.

The first two lines of our chart looked like the one below:

| Aspect | Where We Came From | Where We Are | Where We Are Going |
|--------|--------------------|--------------|--------------------|
| Speech |  |  |  |
| Grouping |  |  |  |

### Grading and Evaluation

In applying dynamic planning and management to grading, the teachers in my group and I realized that most students are accustomed to being graded but have no specific sense of why they receive the marks they do. In planning to eliminate grades (or at least make them more comprehensible) we talked about explaining to students explicit criteria for good, mediocre and bad papers. These standards would include such specifics as having an idea well organized and developed, making a character believable, sustaining an argument and being sure ideas flowed aesthetically.

For purposes of evaluation, I clearly separate writing content from spelling and handwriting. I don't want students to confuse or equate them. I have found it possible to set up multiple ways of evaluating a paper. One would be for spelling; another, handwriting; a third, writing. A crucial point, however, is to be sure that you don't make writing less important than the other two elements.

My dynamic management goal for evaluation of any work is to move from traditional grading to self-evaluation, peer evaluation, and joint critical analysis by teacher and student. There is no better way to move toward this goal than to have students read each other's work and become accustomed to giving constructive criticism. This analysis is not only a way of having students grade themselves, but is also an aid to help them pinpoint aspects of their work that should be revised.

I have found that a manager of a dynamic learning system has to engage in constant program evaluation. You can't depend on testing or any kind of grading to provide the kind of information that will help you know when to change or modify things or when things are going along well.

I continually evaluate my programs informally. I set up an accordion file with the name of a child on each of the sections. I also carry 3″ × 5″ index cards in my pocket and when I notice something that isn't working well or seems to be leading the class to a new stage of development I write it down. Some cards go into individual student files. Others go into a general file that I keep for myself. Over the weekend I look at all the cards. This process often gives me a sense of what planning I need to do for the next week. Typical cards might read:

"John looks ready to break through. He writes and writes."

Rebecca is having trouble with her characters. Get her a good book."

"At reading Tosha said she is bored with my stories. Wanted to read hers to class. Good time to start students doing readings."

"Things seem boring, time to introduce new material. How about mythology, or maybe a publishing project?"

I supplement these notes to myself with another file I keep on each child. When I was a full-time classroom teacher, each week I put one writing sample as well as one math paper in each child's file. I also had the students keep a record of the titles and authors of the books they read and notes on the kind of writing they were doing and thinking of doing.

My students helped me with record keeping. Since letter or number grading was not involved, we would occasionally look at all the files as a group and see what the class as a whole was doing. My goal was to involve students in planning and feedback as much as possible and to help them understand that during the year we would be growing and changing. I wanted them to have the chance to see their own progress.

### Preparing to Write

Outlining is another aspect we considered. We felt that most of our students had been accustomed to being asked to set up an outline for papers they would write and then stick to those outlines. Recognizing that most good writing doesn't work that way, we decided we wanted to help our students take a more flexible approach.

We decided to explain that a writer can just as well begin with an idea, a sketch or a pocketful of notes as a tentative outline. To help the students learn to choose a method of planning that is appropriate to the work they have in mind, we decided to try some traditional aids.

Some of our strategies included having students keep writers' notebooks on ideas to use, sketch their ideas informally and look at actual manuscripts showing writers' work (the *Paris Review* interviews with writers are marvelous sources for this), as well as making rough outlines. From these they can go on to a formal outline if that is the technique that works best for them.

This approach to preparing to write presents a management problem. At what point do you encourage a student to make a clear outline? How does writing get transformed from notes in a writer's notebook to actual composition? I've found that it's important to talk with students about the various ways of planning a piece of writing.

Also, I have found that small management charts of their own that document the stages of their various works have helped many of my students. Remember that you can bring all subject-area writing into a writing program. Here's a copy of the chart that my students use. You can modify it according to how you approach outlining in your class:

| Managing My Writing | | | State of Development | | | |
|---|---|---|---|---|---|---|
| Subject/Theme | Notes | Research | Sketch | Outline | Draft 1,2,3 | Revision Finishing |
| | | | | | | |

## Revising

Revisions, our next consideration, are also a problem for many students, and developing a sense of how to make positive changes takes time. Most students confuse corrections with revisions. Therefore, it's important that they understand that corrections are basically small matters, such as spelling and sentence structure, and that revisions involve larger structural issues of writing. Examples would be developing a character or changing the tone of a piece. A flexible program will enable you to start with minor corrections, and gradually raise questions of style, flow and argument.

A good way to introduce the revision process is to have the students start with very short pieces. You might even write a few bad pieces yourself and work with the class on revising them. You can also give students samples of revisions and show them how writing progresses from a rough draft to a finished product. The goal in the case of revisions is to enable students to recast and perfect a piece of writing.

Here's a selected bibliography of materials showing drafts of written work:

*How I Work as A Poet and Other Essays/Plays/Stories,* Lew Welch (Grey Fox Press, Bolinas, CA 1973)

*The Poet and the Poem,* Judson Jerome (Writer's Digest, Cincinnati, OH, 1974)

*Mystery Fiction Theory and Technique,* Marie F. Rodell (Duell, Sloan and Pearce, New York 1943)

*Contexts of Poetry,* Robert Creeley (Audit/Poetry Inc., Buffalo, NY 1963)

*Context of Poetry: Interviews 1961–1971,* Robert Creeley (Four Seasons Foundation, Bolinas, CA 1973)

*One Half of Robertson Davies,* Robertson Davies (Penguin Books, London 1977)

*On the Poet and His Craft: Selected Prose of Theodore Roethke,* Ralph J. Mills, Jr. (Editor) (University of Washington Press, Seattle, WA 1974)

*How To Write,* Gertrude Stein (Something Else Press, Inc., West Glover, VT 1973)

*Writing Well,* Donald Hall, (Little, Brown and Co., Boston 1973)

*ABC of Reading,* Ezra Pound (New Directions Publishing Corp., New York 1963)

*Writing a Novel: Some Hints for Beginners,* Dorothy Bryant (Ata Books, Berkeley, CA 1978)

*Self Portrait: Erik Blegvad,* Erik Blegvad (Addison-Wesley Publishing Co., Reading, MA 1979)

*Variations on a Theme (An Essay on Revision),* Diane Wakoski, Sparrow 50, Black Sparrow Press, Chicago, November 1976)

*The Poet in the World,* Denise Levertov (New Directions Books, New York 1973)

*Children's Writing: A Sampler for Student Teachers,* David Holbrook (Cambridge University Press, New York 1967)

*Writers as Teachers/Teachers as Writers,* Jonathan Baumbach (Editor) (Holt, Rinehart and Winston, New York 1970)

*Teaching and Writing Popular Fiction: Horror, Adventure, Mystery and Romance in the American Classroom,* Karen M. Hubert (Teachers and Writers Collaborative-Virgil Books, New York 1976)

*The Poetry Connection: An Anthology of Contemporary Poems With Ideas to Stimulate Children's Writing,* Kenneth Gensler and Nina Nyhart (Teachers and Writers Collaborative, New York 1978)

*Rose, Where Did You Get That Red? Teaching Great Poetry to Children,* Kenneth Koch (Vintage Books, New York 1974)

*Writing: A Sourcebook of Exercises and Assignments,* Gunther, Marin, Maxwell, Weiss (Addison-Wesley Publishing Co., Menlo Park, CA 1978)

*I Write What I Want,* Floyd Salas (Poetry in the Schools, Sacramento, CA 1974)

*The Young Writer at Work,* Jessie Rehder (Odyssey Press, Inc., New York 1962)

*Errors and Expectations: A Guide for the Teacher of Basic Writing,* Mina P. Shaughnessy (Oxford University Press, New York 1977)

*Imaginary Worlds: Notes on a New Curriculum,* Richard Murphy (Teachers and Writers Collaborative, New York 1976)

*A Day Dream I had at Night Teaching Children to Make Their Own Readers,* Roger Landrum and Children from P.S. 1 and P.S. 42 in New York City (Teachers and Writers Collaborative, New York 1974)

*The Whole Word Catalogue (Vol. 1 & 2),* (Teachers and Writers Collaborative, New York 1972)

*Just Writing Exercises to Improve Your Writing,* Bill Bernhardt (Teacher and Writers Collaborative, New York 1977)

*The Art of Writing,* Sir Arthur Quiller-Couch (Capricorn Books, New York 1961)

*From Elfland to Poughkeepsie,* Ursula K. Le Guin (Pendragon Press, Portland, OR 1975)

### Style and Voice

Finally, for style and voice I have students begin with imitation and voiceless writing. By "voiceless" I mean objective rather than personal writing. The development of style and voice is a complex matter, so a good first step in introducing these elements to students is to read them and have them consider the styles and voices of classic authors. After listening to and trying voiceless writing and style imitations for a while, they'll be ready to write in their own voices and create their own style.

Below is the rest of the writing program chart we developed:

| Aspect | Where We Came From | Where We Are | Where We Are Going |
|---|---|---|---|
| Grading | | | |
| Outlining | | | |
| Revising | | | |
| Voice and Style | | | |

## The Whole Program

Planning and dynamic management can keep a complex program understandable, under control and productive. Goals are articulated; student status and progression are carefully analyzed and strategies are developed to move students toward more open and intricate writing forms over the course of a school year. The dynamic writing program can be applied to math, reading, or any other subject. The key to creative management is accepting the notion that space, time, content and organization must change as the children grow.

# B
# *The Importance of Writing Every Day*

A plea, with practical suggestions, for making writing, the third R, as central as reading and arithmetic, and an emphasis on daily writing practice.

*I* ran into a former pupil the other day. He was in my class when he was twelve and now he's about to graduate from college. We started reminiscing about our days together in the sixth grade and I asked him whether he felt that anything we did together was of value in his life these days. He said that the personal things were too difficult to evaluate but that one very specific thing we did was functional on an everyday level. That was our fifteen minutes of writing which enabled him to write and rewrite stories and poems and essays without panicking or worrying himself into being dysfunctional. Most of the other students in college looked at writing papers or exams or stories as major crises in their lives. They just didn't know how to go about writing anything and usually tried to produce a finished product the first time around and ended up frustrated and angry about their results.

I remembered my own college days and how much trouble I had writing a paper. Of course, he was right. Every time I had to produce a paper I would wait until the last minute and force myself to stay up all night and type the paper while composing it. Usually I got done about 8:30 in the morning, a half hour before the paper was due. I also remembered that I couldn't reread my own work. Writing was a problem until I decided to start all over again after I graduated from college and write for myself and worry about other people's judgment after I had a chance to rework what I had done and was pleased with it myself. I learned that it was necessary to accept the fact that one had to start out writing badly in order to learn how to write well. It is still the case for me after having written more than a dozen books. The first draft is always full of mistakes, awkward language. It is what I do afterwards that makes the book.

What was of value to my former student was that he wrote in class every day on a wide range and variety of topics. Some I gave him, some he made up himself, some he borrowed from other students in the class. His work was not graded. I read it when he asked, and he rewrote only those things he liked enough to want to perfect. In other words he taught himself to write in a natural and easy way which turned writing into an extension of his spoken voice.

I believe that every class could have a writing program which encourages students to write as they talk—naturally, with energy, and with the freedom to make errors and speak in their own voices. I also feel that in order for a program of this sort to develop the teacher has to write as well as the students and share bits of her writing with the students in the same way that they are expected to share their work with the teacher. It should be like a conversation where the issue of grades is not present.

There are a number of ways to institute a writing program. With very young children the simplest way is to compose collective stories with the class and ask them to illustrate and copy the stories. For example one can begin:

> One day a wild . . .
> I was crying because . . .

I found it most fun to ask the children to begin the stories themselves and take turns finishing. There is always someone who has a story in mind and I put on the board what the children say as they say it.

It is important with really young children to remember how much they can write physically. A story of a few sentences at the beginning of the first grade makes more sense than one of seven or eight lines which the students could certainly compose but not write.

Collective writing with the whole class is only one way to have daily writing. Another way is to have a range of writing possibilities available to the class and during a certain time let the students choose how they want to write for that day. Here are a number of possibilities:

1. Diary writing.

2. Collective writing with a small group of friends. Three or four students who pool their language ability can stretch out much farther than some individuals. There is nothing wrong with encouraging small groups to write one book together, or to get together and help each other write their own books. There is no such thing as cheating in this context. If one person knows how to spell a word or has a good idea on how to end or illustrate a story it should be shared to everyone's benefit.

3. Bound and stapled books. It pays to make little books for students to fill up and to have crayons and magic markers and pencils and stencils around. Students will quickly figure out ways to make their own books and fill up space. They just need to know that you will give them all the words they don't know. I've spent hours simply standing at the chalk board and writing down words students asked for while they were writing their books.

4. A box of starters is helpful for students who don't seem to know how to get started. In the box can be a number of starting themes, some interesting pictures, cut outs of comic book characters, samples of books written by other students.

5. A comic book-making center with blank comic books, some commercial comic books, and a sample of the kinds of balloons and marginal comments that are usually used in comics.

6. Here's a list of fifteen other forms of writing that can be integrated into a daily writing program:

> letters to friends, historical and imaginary people;
> invitations and greeting cards;
> business cards, serious and comic;
> product advertisements and commercials;
> public announcements and posters;
> classified ads;
> how-to-, instructional, and recipe writing;
> interviewing people and transcribing and editing the interviews;
> scripting for plays, radio drama, films, puppet shows, and so forth;
> writing of short forms such as proverbs, fables, and jokes;
> diaries and journals, real and imaginary;
> biography and autobiography;
> travel diaries and travel itineraries;
> study of alphabets, play with letter forms, and the creation of alphabet books;
> book blurbs and cover jacket notes.

You might have noticed that all of this material is teacher prepared. There is no need for commercially packaged materials to develop a daily writing program. There are some useful resources such as the *Whole Word Catalogue* and other material from the Teachers and Writers Collaborative. But the most useful material will be that produced by yourself and your students. It makes sense to provide time for the children to read each other's work and for you to read your work to the class, and, it makes sense to treat writing as a basic skill and have students write at least fifteen minutes a day every day.

# C
# A Closer Look at Revisions and Corrections

Suggestions for integrating corrections and revisions into the process of creation, beginning with developing ideas and including rough writing, revisions, and the development of a polished work.

*J*ames, a fifth grader I have been working with for a few years, is serious about writing. He has written several long science fiction stories as well as a short adventure novel. During one of our first sessions together he asked me when (while writing) he should worry about spelling, punctuation, and quotation marks. At first I didn't understand what he meant. But he explained that there are ideas speeding through his head when he's working on a story, and he wants to write them all down quickly. He said he often needs words he can't spell and this worries him. After a while, the spelling and ideas begin to get confused and he feels like giving up on his work. He wanted to know what to do to get all the ideas the way he wants them in his story *and* have the spelling right.

I encouraged James to think about his writing as a process involving the following three steps:

1. Getting ideas, feelings, or a story down on paper.
2. Rereading the material and working on voice, tone, and continuity.
3. Polishing the work so that it can be read by the people he would like to have read it.

To help James understand this writing process, which I use myself, I set up a series of exercises for him under the condition that he would write everyday. I also agreed to do the same thing myself.

I use these same exercises with my classes and have found them effective in helping the students learn how to rework their writing and see why corrections and revisions are valuable.

Writing every day provides material for revision and correction. At the end of each week James (and other students I work with) agreed to reread their week's work and pick out one example that seemed most worth preparing for others to read.

Getting students to really think about their writing and choose an example they feel good about has helped develop a willingness to deal with grammar and spelling. When students have decided on a particular piece of work they want others to read and they aren't required to correct everything they ever write, the notion of proofreading and revising seems to make more sense to them. The work is no longer simply a practice exercise or the result of following directions from a textbook.

I chose a joke to rewrite and James chose a horror story. Thinking of our potential readers and rereading our work we realized that my joke and James's story did need work.

### Tone, Voice, Continuity

To clarify the second stage of writing—paying attention to voice, tone, and continuity—James and I took turns reading our chosen writings out loud, keeping these questions in mind: Who is telling the story? How does he or she sound? Does the narrative make sense?

James's story had a lot of dialogue, and as he read it he realized how difficult it was to keep track of who was speaking. He admitted that one part of his story had so many quotes that even he had forgotten who was talking. I suggested he take a blue pencil and mark "confusing" on his copy wherever he thought it was unclear. Then I showed him other kinds of notes I make to myself when I reread my work.

I've found that using a blue pencil over my original writing, which is black, clearly separates my editorial comments from the original text and makes rewriting easier. After James went through his text with a blue pencil, he said that this process of judging his own work was more interesting and helpful to him than any comments or grades he had received on previous writing.

There were serious problems with my joke, too. I had tried to write down a Yiddish joke that I've told friends a thousand times. After I had read my written version of the joke, James asked me to tell it. He thought the telling was funny, but not at all like the story I had written. My translation of the telling into writing had made the joke seem pointless and unfunny. There was something in the inflection and gesture I used to tell the story that didn't come across on the written page.

My writing attempt didn't work, but it did help to call James's attention to voice and tone as central elements in writing. Writing down tales, jokes, riddles, bedtime stories, and fairy tales and then reading them aloud is a wonderful way to call young people's attention to the differences between writing and talking, introducing the idea that they are separate crafts.

After James and I read and marked our papers, we rewrote them. He worked to make his story line and dialogue more clear and I tried to make my joke funny. I didn't succeed to my satisfaction, but he did a fine job. He added more description of the thoughts and feelings of his characters and eliminated some unnecessary talk. In general, his revised version seemed to have a reader in mind, while the original was more of a free-flowing dialogue.

### Spelling, Grammar, Punctuation

After we read our revisions to each other, we moved on to the third step. We looked at our second versions for spelling mistakes and obvious errors in punctuation. We also talked about some grammatical issues like the agreement of verbs and nouns in a sentence. At this point my role as a teacher was crucial. Though I had made occasional spelling mistakes and recognized them, James had a limited sense of his errors in spelling and grammar. Since a feeling for proper form in language develops more from extensive reading than from memorization, he hadn't had time to develop an intuitive sense of where the errors occurred.

James and I went over his errors, and at each point I asked him whether he wanted spelling and grammar to be usual or unusual. I explained that in writing dialogue he had the freedom to make his characters speak with a style, character, and rhythm of his own, as long as he was aware of his reasons for doing it.

In a specific instance, one of his characters said, "I ain't go to your castle. It is too mysterious and strange."

I told him that I thought the quote was unnatural—that the two sentences seemed to be spoken by two different people, and "ain't" and "go" didn't seem to fit with each other. We read the sentence aloud several times and James talked about the character he wanted to create. After awhile, he decided on the quote, "I ain't going. It's too scary. That castle is mysterious." James had begun to listen to his own voice and weigh and balance how he wanted his characters to sound. He was accepting the help I could give him and was taking responsibility for correcting his work.

Finally, I typed up all the drafts of James's story and my joke and used them as an introduction for the children I'm working with on writing. My students express the same anxieties in dealing with content, voice, and spelling and grammar that James had. They have little or no opportunity to see drafts of writers' work and usually after examining an original draft and some of its revisions they write more interesting material and feel curious and more confident about technical matters of writing. The process of turning writing into a series of approximations, through experimenting and reading, rereading and revising, is one way of integrating creative writing with the acquisition of some of writing's basic technical skills.

# D
# No More Handsome Princes: How to Develop Voice and Character

On making the tone of your writing attractive or challenging, and on developing interesting characters.

*T*hese days I work with a group of about 50 young writers and eight of their teachers from eight elementary and junior high schools in our area. We meet once a month with each of the schools, as well as the Coastal Ridge Center, taking a turn at hosting. You might call us an intermural literary group.

The students and teachers travel to and from the meetings on school buses and do resemble athletic teams and their coaches riding from school to school to participate in sporting events. In fact, our project began because of a concern that students in our area only interacted with youngsters from other schools in the competitive atmosphere of athletics or possibly a debate at the high school level. A group of other teachers and I wanted to try bringing together younger students of different ages and from different schools to work cooperatively to produce something tangible.

There are many possibilities for cooperative work. Schools can plan and hold joint science fairs or develop interschool theater or even a circus troop to tour and perform at schools and in the community. Music and the visual arts can also provide a focus for cooperative activity among schools. We decided on the joint production of a literary magazine for our first cooperative intermural learning program for several reasons. First, our center and two of the schools involved have small printing presses, and we think that we can typeset and print the magazine ourselves. Also, a number of the teachers know how to bind books. An added strength will be the participation of the county Poetry in the Schools program, which several of our schools work with.

We have held several meetings. Some of the things we have done or plan to do at future meetings—besides helping students plan and produce the magazine—include providing opportunities for students to read their work to each other; bringing in local writers to talk about and read their own works; and presenting seminars on writing, printing, layout and design, and bookbinding. After we've held several sessions we'll begin devoting some time at each meeting to our joint project. Right now, however, we are experimenting with writing techniques and styles.

## First Paragraphs

During one of our first meetings I taught a writing seminar for a group of 16 people ranging in age and experience from fifth graders in school aides and teachers. My topic for the two-hour class was "What goes into the writing of the first paragraphs of a novel." I wanted the group to focus on the introduction of characters and the importance of capturing the reader's interest at the beginning of a book.

To explain what I had in mind, I read the beginnings of a number of novels of recognized merit. These included *A Tale of Two Cities, Hard Times, Catcher in the Rye, War and Peace,* and *Brave New World.* I also read some character descriptions from these books. After talking about the various techniques and carrying on some discussion, I asked everyone to write the first few paragraphs of a novel they would never finish. Since time was limited, I gave them a few specific instructions to help them get started. I suggested that the story either be historical and have taken place at least 100 years ago, or that it begin like the diary of a fictional character created by the author. I also said that I wanted them to pay particular attention to the introduction of the characters. With these suggestions, everyone succeeded in beginning a novel.

When they had finished, people took turns reading their creations. At this time some of the problems associated with introducing characters immediately became clear. Though much of the writing contained wonderful images and the potential for real, not just imaginary novels, none of the characters were described in careful enough detail to seem real. In fact, rather one-dimensional characters—handsome princes, beautiful princesses or nurses, wicked dukes and stepmothers, a few space heroes who were also either handsome or beautiful—populated my students' introductions.

## Casts of Characters

My experience with that seminar led me to develop a series of exercises that concentrate on characterization. In our next meetings we'll begin this minicurriculum, which might be called "No More Handsome Princes." So far, I have tested the material with some success on myself, my own children, a few of their friends and several of the teachers I work with. You might like to try it yourself and add to it. Here are the five basic assignments:

1. Rewrite "Once there was a handsome prince" into a detailed description of a person who could also be a handsome prince. However,

don't use the word *handsome* or any of its synonyms. Instead, let your reader see, and really know, that prince. Your description might be several paragraphs, even several pages, long.

Before you start to write, think about the prince. How does he walk? What does his voice sound like? What is his hair like? How does his face look? Imagine details, such as the shape of his nose or his hands. Visualize the way he eats or says hello, the way he expresses anger or affection. Since this prince is human, as well as handsome, what are his imperfections? Is there anything ugly or mean about him?

2. Rewrite "Once there was a beautiful princess" in the same way you rewrote the sentence about the prince. This time try some ways of describing the person through the eyes of an observer. What are the details of beauty? Are they manifest in the way a person talks or walks or looks? Are there other ways to describe beauty? For example, can you describe the beauty of a person who is also a princess through the way other people react to her? Here's one possibility: "As soon as she entered the room I lost my concentration. I couldn't keep my eyes on my computer, though I love the machine. It was that slightly sad smile she had or maybe the way she seemed to fill up the room with her confidence . . ."

3. Rewrite "Once there was an ugly duke," and try to describe an unattractive person in a way that makes him unique, like no other person alive or imagined. Try to find some beauty in the duke's ugliness. Is there nothing attractive about the people you conceive of as ugly? Do they like their parents? Do they have friends? Enjoy any innocent pleasures? Is ugliness made beautiful by decent actions? What is it that makes people think of some human characteristics as ugly?

Ugliness and beauty are mysterious in a way. No one really knows why some faces are attractive and others not, or whether attraction is universal or determined by your culture and family. Try to make your description one of an ugly/handsome person or an ugly/beautiful one. Make your descriptions particular so that your reader will realize that person has conflicting characteristics.

4. Finish one of the sentences "Once there was an evil . . ." or "Once there was a good . . ." How do you show virtue or evil in a character without simply saying he or she is good or bad and hoping your readers believe you? In life ugliness, evil, beauty, and goodness are mixed in very complex ways. How do you make evil convincing in writing? Is it ever unmixed and absolute? Or are there times when even your evil prince is kind to a dog or sad at the death of a friend?

The complexity of your characters makes your story more alive. The more you see them in depth, the more convincing a story you might write. Know and imagine more about your characters than you will ever write about them.

5. Try these additional exercises after you've finished writing about the handsome prince, the beautiful princess, and, the ugly and/or evil character.

> Describe a meeting between the princess and prince from the point of view of your third character.
>
> Write the thoughts of the prince when he sees the evil or ugly person pass by the princess's house.
>
> Write the princess's thoughts as she compares in her mind the other two characters.
>
> Describe a meeting of all three characters, including their dialogue if you like.

All of these exercises help develop a written voice of interest and character. The voice a person uses in writing is as important as any other single aspect of writing. I remember a number of years ago reading selections from Hemingway, Faulkner, Mann, and Hesse to a number of fifth, sixth, and seventh graders. I asked the students to listen to the selections in order to discover the voice of the author instead of the plot or the characters.

Then I asked the students to imagine that the room we were in was dislocated, that we were spinning in space and that all of a sudden we landed . . . and opened the door to the room. I then asked them to write a description of what they saw.

All but two of the students began writing immediately. One girl said she didn't feel like writing, that there were other more important things on her mind and that she couldn't concentrate. She asked if she could just sit and watch and I told her of course she could.

Another student, a boy, sat on the floor with the rest of us and played nervously with his pencil. There was sweat on his forehead, and it was obvious that he was experiencing extreme anxiety. When I asked him what the matter was he said he just couldn't write, although he wanted to. He didn't know how to begin.

I suggested he free associate, put down any words that came into his mind. I also explained how difficult it often is for professional writers to get started. A blank piece of paper is a very threatening object; it is such an open invitation to create, yet it gives no clues as to how to begin.

The rest of the students finished their papers. Some were several pages long, others only a few sentences. One was a poem. I asked each student to read his paper and explained that there would be no grading. I also explained that learning to write well often involves writing poorly for awhile. There is no point to grading or condemning bad writing. There is, nevertheless, a reason for working on it. Writing well is discovering one's own best written voice and is a part of the more general adventure of discovering oneself. It is not easy, and it takes time and work.

No one volunteered to read. Everyone looked away from me, refusing to engage eyes. They were all trying to hide. I got the feeling that they felt I intended to humiliate them. I asked again and one girl said she couldn't read her piece because her writing had to be awful. Some of the others muttered their agreement. Almost without exception these students were convinced that they could not write well. They were tearing themselves down. They were frightened of their own voices. The next stage obviously would be that they would hate to write and only do it when forced. It was a boring chore that frightened them.

I pushed and finally got one student to agree to read. Before she began I asked the class to listen not to the words or the grammar or the ideas but to the voice of the author. We listened.

> *A plain. Lonely. A man walks across with a stick in his hand. He looks around. Nothing. Nothing. Long lonely empty.*

We listened to her voice, to the pleading, to the condensed adjective-less speech and spoke of the style she was struggling to achieve.

Then someone else volunteered to read:

> *Lushness, a smooth shiny water. Animals all about music in the air, sweet harmonious sounds a flowing rippling undulating . . .*
>
> *I can't go on.*

The voice here was quite different and the student couldn't finish the piece because she couldn't sustain the tone. We talked about the voice in this short piece and how it seemed artificial, what the teacher might want because it used many big words and expressed a positive happy attitude. The voice the student chose trapped her into being artificial. She was trying to figure out what voice would please someone else rather than to discover one of her own.

### Hard Hitting

A third essay was more direct than the other two and hit harder:

*The door opened. Hell! It was the same old crummy world, the dirty streets, the people hanging around drinking shooting stabbing. The room should never have stopped spinning free in space, free at last.*

The students decided that the voice in this piece seemed like the person who wrote it. We talked and talked about voices and all of the students did come round to reading their papers. They began to listen to each other's papers, not to criticize them or place a mark on them or compare them or rate them, but to understand them and learn something about each other.

It is absurd that young people fear their own writing and are ashamed of their own voices. We have to encourage them to listen to themselves and each other, and to take the time to discover who they are for themselves. They should be able to develop their own voices in writing, to experiment with other voices, and through the attention to voice become sensitive to the voices of other people.

# E
# *Writing Poems and Knowing Poetry*

An attempt with the help of several contemporary poets to make clear what poetry is and can be, and to make the writing of poetry a personally engaging and linguistically challenging activity.

*T*here is not much teaching of poetry. Some people teach some poems in their classrooms and have their children do a few exercises that are supposed to generate poems. However, most teachers I know avoid poetry as much as possible and for very good reasons. They don't have any clear definition in their minds of what poetry is. They can't explain the difference between poetry and prose. They don't read much modern poetry. They feel bewildered about how to approach the subject. I felt the same way several years ago and told a friend of mine who was a poet, Muriel Rukeyser, about my desire to teach poetry and my confusion about how to begin or even define the subject for the class. She listened, paused a moment and then handed me a blank piece of paper. "Begin with this and with your student's words. Don't start with definitions, let them emerge."

It hadn't occured to me until then that I could start teaching poetry with the writing of my students, that I could begin without a definition and work towards one by reading poetry myself and helping the students write. Recently I came across a quote by another poet, Wallace Stevens, who said, "One function of the poet at any time is to discover by his own thought and feeling what seems to him to be poetry at that time." Later in the same essay Stevens hazards a guess at what poetry might be. He says it is an unofficial view of being, that it approaches the truth by way of the imagination.

Poets look at poetry as it is being created in the present. They might study the work of the past but their work and their lives are in the present. They don't worry about definitions of poetry the way teachers, who are not trying to make something new, worry about saying the right thing to their students. For that reason what poets have to say about poetry is likely to help us as teachers approach the subject in a fresh way. I asked six poets to tell me how they would explain what poetry was to a student or to a teacher who was curious but not very knowledgeable about poetry. I also asked them what was the difference between poetry and prose, and how they would go about getting someone to write poetry.

### The Poets Talk

Josephine Miles is Professor of English at the University of California, Berkeley. She is a critic and a poet as well as a respected teacher of poets and critics. She explains:

There are many different ways of beginning. If I'm introducing poetry to college students who say, "I've never written a poem and never read any but I'd like to try. . . ." And then I say go ahead and see how it will come out. An imitation of lines like:

> *One morn before me were three fingers seen,*
> *With bowed necks, and joined hands, side-faced;*
> *And one behind the other stepp'd serene,*
> > *In placid sandals, and in white robed graced;*
> *They pass'd like figures on a marble urn,*
> > *When shifted round to see the other side;*
> *They came again; as when the urn once more*
> *Is shifted round, the first seen shades return;*
> *And they were strange to me, as may betide*
> *With vases, to one deep in Phidian lore.*

The terrible thing is that what comes out is a nineteenth century poem. So in college or in any place on any level where a time sense of culture is involved I think the first thing I'd say is go out and read some magazine, some current magazines.

On the other hand there are some students who don't have that sense of what a poem should be. Like this summer I was at the University of Hawaii and everybody told me that this was going to be a very inert, unthoughtful group. They were unprepared in a way but in some way they were more alert to nuances than the people who had grown up in the nineteenth century. So I told the class that I'd be using quite a few words in the next few minutes, words like verse and line and peom, and asked them to stop me "if there's any word you don't understand the meaning of." I told them I didn't want to make any assumptions about what they knew. A student raised his hand and said, "Miss, what's an assumption?" And so stepping back to that I said what an assumption was and then asked "What did you assume poetry was when you came into this class?" And they said, "A Mickey Mouse class." I asked them what was Mickey Mouse about it, and they told me it was because poetry was real easy, that you write it when you're relaxed. This was an interesting dialogue. You really have to find out what the students' preconceptions are. I'm sure this case couldn't be repeated somewhere else. Anyway I asked the class to write something and let me see "what you're assuming this easy stuff is." They wrote jingles and so now I saw what they meant about being easy. It's greeting cards, something like:

> *How wonderful to greet you today*
>   *Now that it is*
>   *The first of May*
> *I hope that you will feel fine*
>   *And not need to depend*
>   *On too much wine*

No, they said its not greeting cards so I asked them to write again. This time they wrote down things like 'what I think is a beautiful word' or something like that. You see they've got a lot of assumptions floating around in there. There's where I disagree with Kenneth Koch and others who try to tell students a poem is like a dream or lie or something like that—that's not them, they may be able to work with that and do beautiful stuff but its by-passing them; it's not where they're at. That's dangerous.

Josephine Miles points poetry back to the self. It is easy to write according to formulas and difficult, even painful, to discover your own voice and a condensed way to express what you feel. Aspects of writing poetry are discovering that personal voice, of molding language to fit your intentions, and of consciously breaking rules to say things with the immediacy and power that images, metaphors, shifts in narrative, and condensed forms can provide.

Not only does one have to worry about assumptions about what poems are. There is a problem with assumptions about what can legitimately be considered poems. Many people have very strong ideas of what poetry isn't. I remember presenting this pop poem by Ronald Gross to a group of students and then another day to a group of teachers:

> *Yield.*
> *No Parking.*
> *Unlawful to Pass.*
> *Wait for Green Light.*
> *Yield.*
>
> *Stop.*
> *Danger.*
> *Narrow Bridge.*
> *Merging Traffic Ahead.*
> *Yield.*

*Squeeze.*
*Dead End.*
*Do Not Enter.*
*Enter at Own Risk.*
*Yield.*
*Yield.*
*Yield.*
*Yield.*

Both groups were equally adament in claiming that it wasn't a poem because it didn't rhyme or have elevated language, and had no relationship, for the most part, to any other poem they had seen. The same thing happened when a number of Black and Puerto Rican poets started writing poetry based in the speech and music rhythms of Afro-American and Afro-Latin music and speech. David Henderson, one of the poets I talked to, has worked in many elementary schools. I asked him to describe some of the problems he faced in trying to change people's concept of what a poem is:

A lot of teachers that I work with assume that they know contemporary poetry. In most cases I feel that isn't true, especially in contemporary Black, Afro-American and Third World poetry which is not based in the classical European style. First I'd try to establish the differences between these traditions by using music, blues and jazz. It's important to talk about tonal language and the oral tradition, and about experiential things that are part of the poetry. I would try to get the teachers to internalize those things, language and the experience of the writers, their protest against colonialism, enslavement.

Students have much less trouble than teachers in internalizing and assimilating Third World and Afro-American poetry since their political and experiential perceptions are much closer to the content of the poetry. Many of the poems are not told straight out. They are told tonally, by the rhythms and the juxtapositions in the images and language. The students can get poems the teacher can't because they know what the poet is talking about. Tonal language talks about a perceptual world which in tonal like blues and jazz and oral poetry. It sings.

When I'm working with a class on my own in a fifth or sixth grade I begin by reading from *The Dream Keeper*, which is the first book of poetry by Langston Hughes. It deals with the kind of perceptions that are not discussed a lot with kids like dreams, little perceptions of everyday things, also issues that deal with the cosmos.

After reading the poems I would encourage the students to talk about their own dreams and their own perceptions and talk about everyday things in their environment. You know that if kids live in a ghetto situation their environment is embarrassing so its touchy. Its hard to get ghetto kids to talk about their everyday lives because they know those are not subjects to talk about at school. I would encourage them to do tonal things. Things that sung. One thing I would not do, that I used to do, was discourage students from writing in couplets, in sincere couplets that sound like a rhythm and blues song. Couplets like:

> *Tired of slippin' and a-slidin' with Long Tall Sally*
> *Peekin' and a-hidin' duckin' back in the alley,*
> *Don't wanna rip it up, don't wanna work with Annie,*
> *I've got a brand new lover, her name is Short Fat Fannie.*

> *One day when I was visitin' at Heartbreak Hotel,*
> *That's where I met Fannie and she sure looked swell;*
> *I told her that I loved her, and that I'd never leave her,*
> *She put her arms around me and she gave me fever.*

I would never discourage students from doing that now. My problem before was that I was thinking of modern poetry and thinking that couplets are out. Since then I've gotten more into music and found that a lot of times a poem will be in couplets and when it is put to music it will come alive.

Asking what is poetry is a little like asking what is music. Think of all the different types of music that you have ever heard. Can you say more than that music is organized sound? And if you try even so general a definition then what can you do with the music of John Cage and other composers who introduce random elements into their compositions. To say that they aren't really music won't do. As the definition of music or poetry or science for that matter is transformed by the work people do in the present we have to learn to expand and change our perceptions of those fields. It is no accident that those children, for example, who have no preconceived notion of poetry can produce work that is interesting and moving. They are not trapped by definitions deriving from what has been done.

John Oliver Simon, a poet with considerable experience teaching young children, described what it's like working with students who are still struggling with learning to read and haven't had much time to worry about poetry.

Last summer I had a class of students that couldn't read. They didn't have an idea of what poetry was. I sat with my typewriter in the center of the room and asked each student to give me a scary thing. As they got excited by their scary things they began to give me a little more and very quickly we had this scary poem. For seven- or eight-year-old kids there is a lot of power in what is scary.

With high school classes where the students have a preconception of poetry, where they usually believe all poems rhyme or all convey insincere emotions, I try to break those stereotypes by reading something of my own or by reading something that other kids have written that speaks powerfully out of their reality. I once had a student who was sent into a poetry class because he was cutting gardening and he had to be sent somewhere. He protested very strongly. He said, "I ain't no fag." That day I brought with me Leesa Felix, a young poet, and she read in class:

> *crazy boy*
> *crazy boy*
> *and who am i to say what crazy means?*
> *who am i to say?*
>
> *daddi looks so tired*
> *hurt in the eyes*
> *pain like nameless ocean*
> *destiny*
> *too clear*
> *mysteries too spoken for*
> *crazy boy*
> *and who am i to say what crazy means?*
>
> *thanskgiving turkey*
> *t.v. dinner style*
> *in san mateo*
> *cheap joint*
> *momi eats plastic pies*
> *swallows them down like eagle*
> *you eat slow*
> *so slow*
> *taste the chocolate you*
> *don't like*
> *oo oo*
> *crazy boy*
> *who am i to say what crazy means?*
>
> *you say you wrote a poem in french*
> *rejected quiet*
> *rejected hurt*
> *your mama always told me you were*
> *too sensitive*
> *for a man*
> *oo oo crazy boy*
> *who am i to say what crazy means?*

*you walk stubborn lost*
*caught in your ideals of*
*space and time*
*leonardo da vinci*
*never showed his secrets*
*hid them in his diary*
*they say he was way ahead of*
*them*
*you know*
*oo oo crazy boy*

Her work was so real to him that he wrote something that was incredibly eloquent even though he could barely read. Now he's planning to be a poet and his reading level jumped five years in six months.

He saw a fifteen-year-old girl who was writing about such things as a suicide attempt and her naked perceptions of her friends and parents—it touched some buzzer in this guy and he could write too.

Recently he told me about a poem he had just written. The last line was 'I don't dream no more' and that's his voice. It has its own powerful rhythm and if he'd been more concerned about being correct and saying "I don't dream any more", which he knows is 'correct', it wouldn't have the same force it does.

That brings me to the difference between poetry and prose. The main difference is that poetry doesn't go all the way across the page. Poetry calls particular attention to what you're trying to say in those choppy units of language that fit on a line. Poetry is broken up in a way that prose isn't, you use language in an intense way that tries to convey strong and immediate feelings. The division between poetry and prose is very fine. A lot of times my students will start off writing all the way across the page and pay no attention to where the line breaks. What I do is type up what they've written but as I type it up I simply go all the way to the end of what they say on the first line—they've created the line breaks by the way they've spoken on the page and I've transcribed it. As we begin to look at what they've done and look at the power of it a kid or two will get the idea of varying off this, of hitting me with a line or two.

Poetry is an open field for thoughts and feelings. The line is the mechanical unit that makes the rest work. The rhythm of a poem should flow out of speech rhythm. Poetry at its best is natural human speech that is heightened.

In the classroom it's important not to worry too much about the formal aspects of poetry and the technique, but to create an atmosphere of trust and confidence where students feel they can share their feelings without too much risk. . . To open up the language so students can express their feelings without worrying about correctness of language or style so that even if what they're feeling is somewhat fragmentary they can feel free to give the fragments rather than agonize over the finished product.

The craft can come later and if a teacher doesn't feel confident to teach it, if they can get the students into the feeling, the pleasure of expressing what's strong for them, then the students can teach themselves form. Most poets always have.

Several years ago John worked in my class for eight weeks and I had a chance to observe him at the typewriter, listening to the students and trying to catch the rhythms of their speech by the way he created line breaks. I tried it with my own speech, taping something and then trying to decide on line breaks and eliminate unnecessary words. Here's one of the efforts.
The way I spoke it:

> *I hate flying, it makes me scared I mean the airplanes and*
> *wondering always where the emergency doors are and if*
> *I'd get out in time.*

Here is my reworking:

> *I hate flying*
> *It*
> *makes me scared*
> *wondering always*
> *where the emergency doors are*
> *and if I'd get out*
> *in time.*

Ishmael Reed, another poet I spoke to, elaborated on the relationship between what is first written.

Poetry comes from the heart—it's like magic and it depends upon sincerity. And on inspiration—if you look at the word—it means seized by the spirit, or inside the spirit, like possession, and it's very difficult to explain what it is, though maybe with the new investigations in parapsychology and physics maybe one day it'll be explained but you just have to have faith that it is there. Young writers, any writers, have to let themselves be seized—write what comes to them, and then they have to learn the tools and techniques that will help them communicate, to be clear—even if you write bizarre stuff, fantasy or new fiction or discontinuous literature—you still have to have craft. You look at Dali, for example, who is considered a surrealist. When you look at his painting you know that he has mastered the tools of painting. He's a great craftsman but his themes are unusual. I think craft and hard work is crucial beyond inspiration. It took me a long time to learn my craft. I wasn't taught that in school. The examples I was given were obsolete. The way in which kids are trained to write like Shakespeare, there's something sick about that. I don't mean the ideas of Shakespeare or the techniques of Shakespeare, the problem is teaching students to write like Shakespeare as if this were Shakespeare's time, using words like "alas." I think it is important that young people see writing as a fine art, that they know there is a craft to it. Then they can write what they want and have to be allowed to write what they want. They can write in any form but they shouldn't be forced to write in Western standards.

One of the problems teachers face is that they don't know all the forms of poetry. When some one says try modern forms and non-Western forms many of us don't have a clear idea of what poets are talking about. And its not our fault. Poetry has been divorced from our everyday experience and we lose a lot because of it. I asked Phillip Lopate, who has worked for the last seven years at P.S. 75 in Manhattan and is a poet and writer, how teachers could approach modern poetry. He said:

If I wanted to get to know modern poetry the first thing I would do would be to go into a bookstore or a library and just start reading poetry. If a poem didn't grab you and you didn't get something from the poet you should leave it at that. I think that people should trust their instincts when it comes to poetry instead of assuming that they're at fault if they don't appreciate something. When you find a poet whose style you like, read everything he or she has written. It's really not important to like all of poetry but it is important to start to trust your tastes in it and use it for your own pleasure.

Then when it comes to introducing your class to poetry I would start with something that was very immediate and hit on their own concerns. I would bring in poems, for instance, that had a narrative line, partly because I like those kinds of poems myself and partly because I'm aware that children are very attracted to stories and are often turned off by poetry because they assume that poetry is only meditative and has nothing to do with stories. When I was a kid the first thing I ever read was Alfred Noyes's *The Highwayman*. I used to make my mother read it again and again because I loved the story of it. To me it was all the better because it was a rhyming story and it had metrical flashes that I could remember.

So I try to read poems to kids that have stories or situations, that deal with people interacting with each other. You can use Theodore Roethke, Charles Reznikov, Anne Sexton, Langston Hughes, even Robert Frost poems, but somehow get the students inside a restaurant or schoolhouse or get them a scene which deals with family. For instance I read this poem by Anne Sexton about the first time she ate oysters with her father, and then there's that poem by Theodore Roethke, *My Papa Waltz*. Starting with things in the family has always attracted me because already there are characters and situations and constancy. I would like students to see poetry as something that churns up their guts, which involves very important relationships. Poems that begin with lines like these written by Charles Reznikov are good:

Their new landlord was a handsome man. On his rounds to collect rent she became friendly.

Or:

When he was four years old, he stood at the window during a thunderstorm. His father, a tailor, sat on the table sewing.

Or:

When the club met in her home, embarrassed, she asked them not to begin: her father wanted to speak to them.

I think it might be interesting to approach the question "what is poetry" head on. For me poetry is always in the process of becoming. It is not something which is fixed but something which is historically changed and which partly depends upon what the poet chooses to define as poetry. Part of what has happened in the twentieth century is that poets have tried to get down to the root element of poetry by stripping it of some of the decorative elements which were always thought to be its essence. Writing poetry is a continuous looking for the essence of poetry and what I would do with students is try to define what a poetic state is, what a poetic mood is even if it doesn't result in poetry. For instance, you might be walking around and looking at everything and it might have a kind of luminosity to it or a specialness to it—you would be in a poetic state even it no poem came out of it. I think there is a condition of poetry which is like a spiritual state, and then there's the product and the craft of poetry which is something else.

At this point I asked Phillip if there was any difference between prose and poetry and he answered:

"I would say, laughing while I said it, that one of the differences between poetry and prose is that prose tends to have a right-hand justified margin* (at least when it's typeset by people who have some money) and poetry tends to have uneven right-hand margins. Poetry tends to exploit the spaces between lines and the length of a line more than prose does. However you can't just say that poetry is more condensed than prose because there are a lot of prose writers like Isaac Babel who write extremely condensed prose and a lot of poets like Allen Ginsberg who write florid and expansive poetry. I also think that if you look at

---

*A justified margin is one in which the print lines up straight down the page. With an ordinary typewriter it is easy to have a justified left hand margin but practically impossible to get a justified right margin. Look at a paper you wrote for some college class. You'll see that the type on the right hand side does not line up down the page. This is called a ragged margin. The type in this book is justified both left and right.

American writers like Melville and Hawthorne both of them have prose styles which have very strong metrical bases. You could practically scan Melville's books as iambic pentameter.

So what distinguishes poetry isn't the metrics of it . . . it's almost the fastidious attitude towards space and the arrangement of words on the page. It's using that visual factor that prose uses only by paragraphs and chapter breaks that makes poetry. Poetry has certain tendencies too, like crystallization and condensation, the ability to say more in fewer words, a rhythmic underbase, sometimes forms like sonnets and villanelles which it doesn't have to use but still has available.

I write poetry and prose and sometimes I'm faced in a direct manner with the challenge of whether to write something as a story or an essay or a poem. At times I've actually written something out in prose and decided it would make a better poem and sometimes vice versa. One way to find out the difference between poetry and prose is to take the same idea and the same content and try to express it both ways. When you do that you often find that poetry leads you into a more quirky, imagistic approach to language and that prose is more discursive. The same idea can be handled differently.


Hank Heifetz who is also a novelist and a poet has a specific way of defining what a poem is. According to him:

A poem is a rhythm that expresses a feeling. It can be a feeling about ideas or events, or it can be a feeling that is an emotion. The best way to get students to see that is to have them write down short passages about something that's affected them and then show them when the emotion has clearly taken over the words and has embodied itself in the rhythm of the writing. This passage itself without breaking it up into lines can be taken as a poem. But very often because the stress of emotion has shown itself in certain words you can take a little thing of four or five lines which is written in prose and show someone who isn't used to the idea that he or she has written a poem, that this is indeed a poem. If you break it up in a certain way by making lines out of it, you can make something that is more effective than the prose. That's the way to get people to learn what the poetic line is from the inside. A poem is a confrontation with some reality, something you're trying to produce. It is an attempt to provide rhythmic access to your own unconscious. A poem is like a statue cut out of your mind, a mixture of conscious and unconscious decision.

Rhythm is very basic to any kind of writing and living. For example when you're taken over by an emotion your breath changes, and when you're writing a poem that comes out of a real feeling—say hatred—the rhythm of the words is very akin to yourself as you breathe in a state of hatred.

Music is very useful in presenting the sense of poetry. It is a good idea to listen to music of some rhythmic complexity when you start to write poetry. Let the music soak into your sensibility. However, make sure that the music doesn't alienate, that it speaks to the students in some way. See what the music sets up in terms of the richness of writing produced.

A poem becomes the living expression moment to moment of that you're feeling.

I like to read to my students. One of the things I always do is read with the proper emotional stress, with the emotional rhythm I see in the poem without holding back in any way. I stress to my students that they shouldn't bother reading poetry if you don't take it in, internalize it, if you don't put your emotions, your past, your life into a poem you care about or that troubles you, read it with that energy aloud or to yourself. Let the poem as an energy field work on you. A poem is basically a concentration, a crackle of energy.

When a poet creates it it's a movement of continually shifting energy in which the line is the basic component. The line is the single most clear element you take into your head, especially in modern poetry. If you move emotion-by-emotion, feeling-by-feeling, using the line as a unit you will experience the continual flow of energy which is a mirror of reality. The most important thing about reading a poem is that it not be approached in a dead manner.

I asked Alta, who is the central figure behind the shameless hussy press as well as a poet and teacher of poetry, to describe some of the specifics of how she teaches poetry. At first she hesitated, since most of her teaching experience is with older people at college and in adult-education classes. However, she agreed to describe what she does and speculate on how it can be used with young children. Alta presented five assignments:

The first assignment I use is to have the students read aloud someone else's work. Their first voice aloud thing is not their own work. They get used to speaking in front of everybody and not being dumped on and being judged. I bring a bunch of things to class for them to read. I've Xeroxed a bunch of things that women have said about writing. I have people take turns reading them aloud. Then:

The next assignment is to read something they've written that is old and hasn't been reworked. Because it hasn't been reworked there's no judgment made on it.

The third assignment is to write down someone else's story. I would do that with young children too. I ask the women in my class to get their mothers or grandmothers or some really older woman seventy years or older and recapture their history. That would certainly work with children. They could go home and ask their grandmother to tell a story and they could write it down or have her write it down. It has to be a story about her life, a true thing—to help get them thinking in terms of the history that's been left out and how we can recapture it.

I don't even mention 'poetry.' My students assume since it's a poetry class that they do little short things but a lot of material they initially come in with is in paragraphs. If at the end of the class they want to, they can hone it down into a poem, that is take out all the words that don't work, all the words you would pad a poem with to make it a prose piece. Then you juggle the lines until the beginning of each line has a purpose for that word being at the beginning of the line.

My fourth assignment is to have the students write down a children's poem. For young children I would ask them to hang around a tiny child, one who is just learning to talk, or a two- or three-year old, and have them write down a few of the things they say. And then I'd ask them to try and remember when they were that age and write a thing of their own as if they were that age.

Finally I ask the students to put together a group of poems into a magazine. I would ask each child to pick five different poems by five different children, poems they liked, and put them together so they would fit into a whole like a magazine does. Five things added together make more than just five separate poems. And then I would have the whole class do a magazine with one piece of work from each child, put it together, write it on ditto masters, do drawings, make it pretty. Then the next thing is to make copies so that everyone can have them and read them.

I hope that the words of these poets will make modern poetry seem more accessible, interesting, and worth teaching. However, the only way to really feel comfortable with poetry is to read and read until you discover what you like. Go to a bookstore and buy a number of anthologies. Jump in and discover if there is anything that moves you.

If you still ask yourself "Why bother? What is the role or function of poetry anyway?" I can only answer with the words of another poet, Jerome Rothenberg:

What do we say about the function of our poetry, the thing we do? That it explores. That it imitates thought or action. That it proposes its own displacement. That it allows vulnerability and conflict. That it remains, like the best science, constantly open to change: to a continual change in our idea of what a poem is or may be. What language is. What experience is. What reality is. That for many of us it has become a fundamental process for the play and interchange of possibilities.

# III
# The Environment: Past, Present, and Future

# A
# *Horizontal History*

An approach to history that studies all the events
in the world at a given date instead of studying
events over a period of time in one place: for
example, studying events over the world in 1492
instead of events in England from 1400 to 1500.
This section gives concrete suggestions on how
to integrate horizontal historical studies into
the more usual vertical studies of history.

*E*nvironmental studies are usually taken to be studies of the present state of our world. But in its broadest conception environmental studies should include history, contemporary studies, and speculations about ways of developing a livable future.

Michel Butor in his novel *Degrees* describes a remarkable history class which could be called 1492A. The class studied what happened in the world during the year 1492. This approach could be called horizontal history rather than vertical history. It sliced across time to take a multicultural perspective on events rather than simply studying the "march of time" leading up to contemporary Europe. From a horizontal perspective 1492 was the year that three small ships crossed from Europe to the American continents and one group of people met another. The Native Americans discovered Columbus just as much as Columbus discovered them.

In 1492 Jews and Moslems were expelled from Spain, the Aztec Empire was flourishing, there was high culture in China, there were wars of conquest and independence throughout the African continent, the Moslem world was expanding, the Ashanti kingdom was stable and powerful. When one looks at the world and not merely at one's own country events take on different meanings. It is no longer easy to tell what was important and what insignificant, what was "progress", what "decadence." From some future world perspective events taking place in China or Central Africa might seem as important as Columbus's voyages.

I find it necessary to remind myself that nations are not eternal. Mozambique is not yet 10 years old as an independent country. The People's Republic of China is thirty years old. However, China as a nation has existed for thousands of years. The Assyrian nation which existed for hundreds of years is no more. It is in the context of the ebb and flow of nations that we ought to consider the two centuries that the United States of America has existed.

I originally wrote this article in 1976 and focused on our national Bicentennial, but any year will do to study horizontal history. Most suggestions for observing the Bicentennial focused on the United States but I suggested it was important to take a wider perspective on our history and that a horizontal approach to the Bicentennial had much to teach us about our role in the world and about the way things change over time. Any year, however, can serve horizontal history as 1976 did for me.

As a beginning it makes sense to focus on three years, centuries apart: 1776, 1876, and 1976, and upon five places in the world. In planning to approach the '76s with a group of third, fourth, and fifth graders, I decided to focus on the United States, China, England, Ghana, and Mexico. The choice was frustrating since India, North Africa, the entire South American Continent, Japan, Canada, and so forth were left out. The places chosen were selected simply because I had access to a lot of material on those places and they were spread throughout the world. If anyone else chooses to do horizontal history, other places will certainly be equally interesting.

Trying to find out what was happening even during one year is an enormous task. Therefore, I had to limit myself again. I asked my students what they would like to learn about the ways other people lived and thought. We came up with this list of questions.

### Growing Up

What was it like to grow up in that place at that time? What games did the children play? How did their parents treat them? How did they dress? Did they work? Did they have to go to school? What did they learn? What were their teachers like?

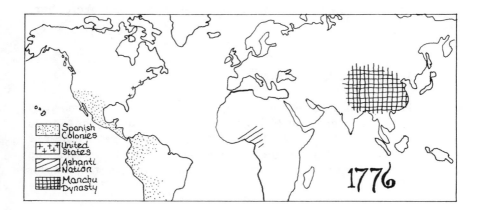

### Eating

What did people eat? Who prepared the food? Did they eat meat? Did they hunt? Were there any vegetarians? Were there restaurants? Who went to them? Did everyone eat the same kind of food? Could we prepare the kind of food they ate? How is like the food we eat? How is it different?

### Singing and Dancing

What kinds of music did people listen to? Who played it? What instruments did people use? Was there a difference between popular and classical music? Were there different kinds of music for different times and places, such as holidays, sports events, dances, concerts, weddings, death? Did most or only a few people play and sing?

### Who Controlled Whom?

Who was the boss in the family? Did the mother and father have the same power or did one control the other? What rights and powers did children have? What kind of behavior was expected of them? At work was everyone equal or was there a boss? Were there many different paying jobs? How did people settle disagreements at work? How was the government set up? Was the country controlled or governed by another country? Was it a democracy? Were there both rich and poor people? How did these groups treat each other? Who made laws and how were they made? How were people who broke the laws punished? Were there jails?

### Who Could Love Whom?

How did people get married? Could they marry anyone they wanted? Did people date much? How much freedom did they have to go out and be together? Were people upset if people from certain ethnic or racial groups or social classes dated or married outside their own group or class? At what age did people generally get married? Was this true for everyone?

### Machines and Moving

What kinds of machines existed? How were they made? Who owned them? How did people make houses? How did they get from one place to another? Where did they live? Were there any big cities? What were they like? Did people stay in the same places all their lives or did they move around a lot?

### A Dual Viewpoint

After discussing these six categories and the questions we had compiled, we talked about the fact that the same questions could be asked about our lives today. History that can be seen from a dual viewpoint seems so much more natural than history that deals with "important" events in the past but never touches on everyday life. It was clear from the questions on our list that my students weren't curious about significant dates or characters, rather they wanted to get a sense of people's lives.

In setting out to answer these questions I realized that, in most cases. I knew as little as the students. I learned history from a vertical perspective and remembered names and dates but knew very little about the lives of people. The attempt to answer as many of the questions as was possible with our resources was as much a learning experience for me as for any of my students.

In order to keep a focus on the complex things we were trying to do we made up the following chart for each country and year we studied:

| Nation | Year | Aspect of History |
|--------|------|-------------------|
| United States | 1776 | 1. growing up |
| | | 2. eating |
| | | 3. singing and dancing |
| | | 4. who controlled whom |
| | | 5. who could love whom |
| | | 6. machines and moving |

As a way of introducing students to the research involved in horizontal history, we all looked at a globe I was lucky enough to have in class, one that did not indicate political boundaries. The globe showed land masses, mountains, rivers, and oceans. Thus, we could pretend that the globe represented the earth before people had spread out.

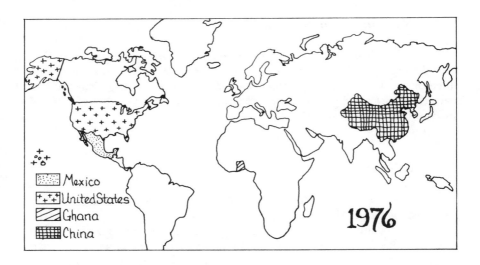

The children immediately saw all kinds of possibilities in dividing the land and the water. One child suggested that every person could have his or her own country. Another mentioned that it might have been possible for no countries to ever exist and for the earth to be one land in which all the people spoke the same language. Then the students made drawings of a number of possible ways the world might have developed or might develop in the future.

### A Change in Plan

When we began to look at what the world was like 200 years ago and today, one student suggested that we also speculate about what it might be like 200 years from now. Originally I had planned to consider 1776, 1876, and 1976 but as a result of this student's suggestion our plan changed to a study of four areas of the world in 1776, 1976, and 2176.

We started with three huge, hand-drawn world maps. I brought in a historical atlas, and we found a map dated 1776 and one for 1974, close enough to 1976 for our purposes. I made sure I explained that the world is changing fast, especially Africa, for example, and that 1974's map wouldn't represent the way things are today. To note more recent changes we discussed the possibility of collecting current-events maps from newspapers and magazines.

As we filled in our maps, the first thing the students noticed was that there was no Mexico, People's Republic of China, or Ghana on the 1776 map. They also noticed that the United States was tiny. Some students seemed to realize for the first time that countries are the creation of people and that they come and go.

Next we tried to answer some of the questions we had raised. First, what was it like to grow up in the United States, the colonies of New Spain, the Ashanti nation and the Manchu empire in 1776? Right away we encountered frustrations. Clearly, our classroom resources would get us nowhere. Neither the history books nor the encyclopedia dealt much with growing up.

As discussion began, we also realized that the question itself was too simple. The students wanted to know whether we were considering boys or girls. One child asked, What about poor children and rich children? And I began to anticipate many other questions. In dealing with Colonial America, What about the children of slaves and Native American children?

### Too Great a Challenge?

Every nation we were to consider would be equally complex and include an overwhelming variety of experiences for all the children growing up in different times and places. The complexity of the subject and lack of resources to cover it became more evident.

At this point I began to wish I had never brought up the idea of horizontal history or thought of dealing with everyday life. As I became more and more discouraged with the task, my students became more and more enthusiastic and fascinated with the idea of such diversity. My first instinct was to pull out, do a year's research on the question myself and then develop the ideas with a class. But I decided to follow the children's energy and go on.

### An Adventure

I also predicted that it would take much longer than we had expected, and, in some cases, we might not be able to come up with all the answers. This intrigued the class even more. It all seemed like an adventure—questions that are puzzles, things adults can't answer, information that has to be dug out. I still had doubts, but these were outweighed by the possibilities that such a study would expose the children to what real scholarship is about and raise questions that they might remember and choose to deal with later in their lives.

Before we could begin a more intense search for resources, we had to refocus our original questions a bit. We decided that for each nation or people we studied, we would try to find out what happened to boys and men and girls and women who were rich, middle class and very poor. We would compare our findings with what we felt to be true or could find out about conditions in 1976 and predict some of the things that might happen by 2176. We would discuss and predict how we ourselves might influence what could happen in the future. We would be sure to try to find out if, in the past, there were any groups within each country that dominated other groups and if there were racial and ethnic differences that influenced the way people were treated and the way children grew up.

### Where to Look

The library was an obvious place to begin. However, there were other avenues that led to equally rich resources: bookstores and record stores; the Mexican and Chinese restaurants in our community, the university, which has several ethnic studies departments; the consulates of the countries we were studying, each of which has a representative in San Francisco, about a half-hour trip for us. There are also community organizations in our local Chicano, Black, Asian, and Native American neighborhoods. Toy stores are another different resource, since many carry games from all over the world.

Thus, 200 years of history began for us with an unexpected exploration of our own community, where many people could give partial answers to our questions. We found out that a number of university students grew up in Ghana, that some of the children in the school had been born and had lived in Mexico, that the grandparents of several Chinese students remembered what a traditional Chinese childhood was like and that some of the children had relatives who still lived in China or Mexico or had been to Africa and learned of their roots. There were also children of pioneer families whose grandparents had all kinds of fascinating and revealing stories to tell. If you try a similar study, you may want to choose countries that fit the backgrounds of your students and/or community.

We never finished our study or came up with complete answers to our questions. However, our project elicited rewards that are different and far greater than I have experienced through studying history in more traditional ways. I feel it was a successful way of avoiding giving young children a false sense of the way things are and have been. Both my students and I have begun to think in new ways.

For other students and teachers willing to embark on a similar open-ended attempt to discover how things happened and are happening in the world, I would like to suggest the following resources, which are organized according to the questions we asked ourselves when we began.

### Learning About Growing Up

*Centuries of Childhood: A Social History of Family Life* by Phillipe Aries (Vintage, N.Y.) is about the origins of the modern family. Although essentially about Europe, it is full of insight about the Colonial American, White family.

*Games and the World* by Frederic V. Grunfeld (Holt, Rinehart) provides illustrations, fascinating historical material, and plans for making inexpensive versions of games and tips on how to use them in the classroom. Two hundred years is a short time in the history of many games, and it is interesting to discover how many games we play were also played 200 years ago.

*Africa Counts* by Claudia Zaslavsky (Prindle, Weber and Schmidt, Boston) contains material about games, riddles, puzzles, and songs of contemporary Ghanaian children. It also refers specifically to games and other aspects of Ashanti life.

*Games and Songs of American Children* (second edition) by William Wells Newell (Dover Books) is a collection of early games and songs of American children of English parents.

*Games of the North American Indians* by Stewart Culin (Dover Books) is an 800-page book full of pictures and drawings and accounts of the games played by native Americans.

Two interesting accounts of growing up that will give young people a sense of what it is like for children to live in the midst of cultural conflict are *The Middle Five: Indian Schoolboys of the Omaha Tribe* by Francis La Flesche (University of Wisconsin Press) and *A Chinese Childhood* by Chiang Yee (W. W. Norton).

### Eating Habits

The best resources concerning how people eat are cookbooks and cooks. Any bookstore has a selection that gives traditional as well as modern dishes. It's especially fun to talk to chefs and other people who prepare food in different styles. It is hard to find much information on traditional food of 200 years ago, but it is possible to learn a great deal by studying native plants and animals. For example, turkey, tomatoes, potatoes, and corn are native to the American continents and therefore, traditional dishes can be expected to contain them. (See "Cooking Up Some History," p. 42. *Teacher*, Feb. '76 for more information on Colonial foods and recipes.)

### Singing and Dancing

The Schwann Record catalogue is a wonderful source for references to music throughout the world, and there are many people who work in record stores who will share what they know about music with you and your students.

The revised Standard Oil School Broadcast series contains a number of extraordinary new records dealing with music. These are available free to schools in the Western States, the Rocky Mountain area, and West Texas from Standard Oil Company of California, Public Relations Dept., 225 Bush Street, San Francisco, CA 94104. They include records on brass instruments, the piano, stringed instruments, the guitar. Each explores a variety of performance styles and cultural traditions. The volume on drums was particularly interesting to us, because one side is devoted to the music and meaning of the Ashanti talking drums.

### The Structure of Society

There are a number of books that give insight into the social and political structure of the societies we are attempting to study. Some of them are: *Imperial China* (Vol. 1 of China Reader Series), ed. by Franz Schurmann and Orville Schell (Vintage imprint of Random); *Inside a People's Commune* by Chu Li and Tien Chieh-yun (Foreign Languages Press); *Muntu: An Outline of the New African Culture* by Janheinz Jahn (Grove); *Custer Died for Your Sins* by Vine Deloria (Avon); *The Myth of the Negro Past* by Melville Herskovits (Beacon Press); *Aztecas Del Norte* by Jack Forbes (Fawcett). The same books that give a sense of power relations also talk of love and the family.

### Machines and Moving

We have found the following books useful as a starting point: *Great Inventions* by Jerome S. Meyer (Pocket Books), *Men of Science and*

*Adventure* by the editors of American Heritage (American Heritage) and *The Way Things Work,* ed. by T. Lodewijk et al (Simon and Schuster).

There are many other resources. Here's a partial list for the places we studied: Ghana, the United States, the People's Republic of China, and Mexico.

### Ghana and the Ashanti

*The Hat Shaking Dance and other Ashanti Tales from Ghana* by Harold Courlander with Albert Kofi (Harcourt, Brace, and World, New York 1957)

*The Cow-Tail Switch and Other West African Stories* by Harold Courlander and George Herzog (Holt, Rinehart and Winston, New York, 1947)

*African Religions and Philosophies* by John S. Mbiti (Doubleday Anchor Book, New York, 1970)

*Games of the World* ed. Frederic Grunfeld (Holt, Rinehart and Winston, New York, 1975)

*African Heroes* by Naomi Mitchison (Farrar, Straus, and Giroux, New York, 1968)

*Africa Must Unite* by Kwame Nkrumah (Heineman, London, 1963, available in the United States.)

### The United States of America

*Roll, Jordan, Roll: The World the Slaves Made* by Eugene Genovese (Pantheon, New York, 1974)

*Ribbin', jivin' and playin' the dozens* by Herbert L. Foster (Ballinger, Cambridge MA, 1974)

*The Myth of the Negro Past* by Melville Herskovits (Beacon, Boston, 1958)

*Games of the North American Indians* by Stewart Cullin (Dover Books, New York, 1975)

*America, A Prophecy* ed. by Jerome Rothenberg and George Quasha (Vintage, New York, 1974)

*Custer Died for Your Sins* by Vine DeLoria, Jr. (Ballantine, New York, 1972)

*The Sound of the City: The Rise of Rock and Roll* by Charlie Gillett (Outerbridge and Dientsfrey, distributed by Dutton, New York, 1970)

### The People's Republic of China

*Report from a Chinese Village* by Jan Myrdal and Gun Kessle (Pantheon Books, New York, 1981)

*China: The Revolution Continued* by Jan Myrdal and Gun Kessle (Random House, New York, 1972)

*Away With All Pests* by Dr. Joshua Horn (Monthly Review Press, 116 West 14th St., New York 10011, 1971)

*Americans and Chinese: Reflections on Two Cultures and Their People* by Francis L.K. Hsu (Doubleday/Natural History Press, New York, 1972)

There are many very interesting books for children published by the People's Republic of China that are available in English translation. These books are available in most stores that sell artifacts and manufactured goods from the People's Republic and are published by the Foreign Languages Press located in Peking. Some of the more interesting ones are: *Monkey and the White Bone Demon; Going to School; Old Tales Retold; Tunnel Warfare,* all published in the People's Republic of China and available in stores that sell Chinese products.

*Mexico*

*Five Families* by Oscar Lewis (Basic Books Paperback, New York, 1959)
*TheMaya* by Michael Coe (Penguin Books, New York, 1980)
*The Aztecs of Mexico* by G. C. Vaillant (Penguin Books, New York, 1955)
*The World of the Maya* by Victor W. von Hagen (Mentor, New York, 1960)
*The Aztecs Under Spanish Rule* by Charles Gibson (Stanford University Press, Stanford CA, 1964)
*A Short History of Mexico* by J. Patrick McHenry (Doubleday, Garden City, NY, 1970)
*The Other Mexico* by Octavio Paz (Grove Press, New York, 1972)
*The Labyrinth of Solitude* by Octavio Paz (Evergreen, New York, 1962)

# B
# Local History:
# Her Story, His Story,
# and Our Story

This section describes ways to develop local history, to use student's family histories in the curriculum, and to integrate the history of women, working people, and minorities into a rounded view of the growth of our nation.

*S*ome years ago, when I was teaching in an all Black elementary school, one of the students walked up to the chalkboard and challenged me: "Mr. Kohl, I dare you to read this!" He then proceeded to write "history."

I knew there was some trick, but let myself be baited and said the word "history," which meant the study of things that happened in the past. He laughed and said that actually it was a misspelled word, it should have read *his*-story—the story of how the past was supposed to be from the perspective of the White man.

I couldn't disagree, since on my desk I had a history book that misrepresented the contemporary United States as a peaceful and perfect democracy and that treated the past history of most of the peoples that make up this nation with scorn and derision. It was as if most of us—Polish and Jewish and African and Mexican and Irish and Italian—had no culture before we arrived or as if those elements of our culture that survived were burdens and signs of inferiority.

More recently a student asked me the same question. She wrote the word history on the chalkboard and explained that the original spelling was indeed *his*-story and that women had been left out. Otherwise it would have been call *her*-story or *our*-story.

### Our Town's Story

The notion of "our-story" fascinated me, and so I decided to pursue it. I suggested that we investigate the past of our community, our families, and uncover the reason Berkeley, California, my home at the time, is the way it is today.

We decided to do some research in the library but the emphasis was on using people's actual experiences and recollections as much as possible. The families and relatives of the students in the class were the logical starting point.

We wanted to ask people questions and gather old documents and materials such as letters, diaries, pictures. We also wanted to tape recollections of earlier times, discover how the community looked fifty years ago and learn what old people thought had changed and what had remained the same.

### Digging for Roots

The class spent a few days discussing what we wanted to discover from our research and what kinds of information would help us most. We then compiled a questionnaire designed to provide us with that information, so we could begin to generate an account of our city's recent past. The students distributed the questionnaire that follows to their relatives and neighbors:

The students in our class are trying to find out about the people in Berkeley and about what the city was like before we were born. We need your experience to help us. Could you answer these questions? If you do not have the time to write your answers, we will be glad to tape them. Thank you.

1. Were you born in Berkeley?
2. If not, when did you come here? What was it like when you arrived? Do you remember any specific things? Do you have things you brought with you? Do you remember your reasons for leaving your old community?
3. If you were born in Berkeley, what was it like then? Where did you grow up? Has the neighborhood changed? What did you do during an ordinary day when you were five years old? Ten? Fifteen? What was going to school like? What games did you play? What dances did you do? What songs did you sing as a young person?
4. What is the oldest thing in your possession? Could we see it, and could you tell us about it?
5. What nursery rhymes did your parents and grandparents recite to you? What childhood dreams do you remember?
6. Who governed Berkeley when you were young? What did people do for a living? Do you have pictures or other things you've saved from the time you were young?
7. What do you remember of other people you grew up with? Are many of them still living here? What were they like, and what are they doing now?
8. Do you remember the oldest people you knew as a child? What were they like, and where did they come from? Do you remember any of their stories?"

The responses to the questionnaries were amazing. It was as if the old people had never been asked to tell what they knew or had experienced or had to teach.

We learned that what is now called Berkeley was once two towns, Berkeley and Ocean View, and that the poorer town, Ocean View, was swallowed by the richer Berkeley. We discovered that Ocean View-Berkeley had been a lumber shipping port and that many Finnish people settled in the town because of the lumbering industry there. Berkeley was identified with the University; Ocean View with the working people in the town—an attitude that still exists today.

We found out where the original town hall and fire station had been located. In fact, they were across the street from where one of the students lived, and she did not know until her grandmother told her.

### Our Family Story

We also found out where most of the students' relatives came from. People had different personal reasons for moving west, but a general discontent with the urban North or rural South emerged as the main reason. People came for a newer, freer life and told us of their hopes and disappointments.

More recent "pioneers" were drawn to the West by the shipbuilding industry that Henry Kaiser developed on the West Coast during World War II. After the war, the industry collapsed leaving many of the migrants in desperate search for new ways to survive.

People in the community showed us photos, letters, and diaries, and told us tales, reflecting on World War II, the Depression, on good and bad times. We had a wealth of material from which we could piece together *our*-story. It became clear to the students that this would be neither one story for all of us nor a simple story for any of us.

Our "firsthand" materials were supplemented with information found in public archives and the university library. A picture began to emerge of a diverse community with conflicts and divisions that still play roles in our everyday lives. Many of the things that had seemed so new to the students and myself were just newer forms of old social and political problems.

### Make a Living Museum

Afterwards there was a discussion about doing something with all the materials we had gathered—showing the community a portrait of itself. We dreamed of creating a living museum from one of the parks or a schoolyard, utilizing our information and the people we had talked to. The plan was to display old photographs, have people teach the games and songs they knew as children, listen to tapes of old stories and display copies of letters and diaries. We also wanted to have different guest speakers from the community talk about their childhood.

In addition, we planned to make a giant map and time line of the lives of the students and their relatives. The map was to be of the world, and we would design it to illustrate our backgrounds as far back as we could trace them. We wanted to surround the map with pictures we had taken of the people in the community juxtaposed with photos from their youth. Our goal was to make the community come alive with a sense of itself. Although we never did it, the idea is something I feel could be attempted by any community in our nation.

Several years after working on this community-history project I visited Eliot Wigginton and Foxfire in Rabun Gap, Georgia.

*Foxfire* (named after a tiny phosphorescent organism) is a student-run magazine dedicated to the collection and preservation of the oral history, folklore and folklife (or traditional culture) of the students' own locality—Appalachian Georgia. Those first youngsters at the Nacoochee School in the Rabun Gap community of North Georgia worked on every aspect of their magazine. Tape recorders and notebooks in hand, they ranged far afield, collecting a wide variety of materials from the living repositories of the old mountain culture. The students organized, transcribed and edited these materials. Then they designed, raised money for, sold and distributed the first edition of *Foxfire*, which came out in early 1967. From this point, the students did their own bookkeeping and kept the "business" going. Though the Foxfire concept has grown and spread, the Foxfire magazine and its offshoots have remained classroom projects, directed and carried out by successive generations of "ordinary" students from Rabun County, Ga. Foxfire is still *their* project.*

The Foxfire idea seemed to have many possibilities for my work and I got excited about having students document the cultural life of their community by talking to older citizens and members of their families. However, my third-to sixth-grade students' situation in Berkeley, California, was quite different from that of Wig's high school students in rural Georgia. Most significantly, there was so much movement in and out of our community that my students had little access to the kind of information about the traditional ways of living and working that the Georgia students uncovered. In fact, most of the families of my students included no more than two generations in the area. On the other hand, we were part of an extremely diverse community. There was no telling what we might find out through some student interviewing.

*From *The Fire that Lit Up Learning* by Thad Sifton *Teacher Magazine* March, 1979 p. 65.

I began by showing a group of fourth, fifth, and sixth graders some copies of the Foxfire magazine and asking them to think about the old people they knew. I was astonished to find that the majority of these students had no idea what their grandparents did and that many of them didn't even know their grandparents' names. As a result, I shifted my line of questioning to ask the students what they might be interested in knowing about older people. The response to my queries was a vast silence. So I tried again, asking the students if they would like to talk to their parents about the the parents did when *they* were young.

That possibility struck a responsive chord, and the students wanted to interview their parents right away. However, having done some interviewing myself and having talked with Wig about the problems that can arise, I insisted that we do some preliminary interviewing in class. Through such practice, students realize how important it is to be prepared to ask interesting questions and learn how to follow up on provocative leads.

To start our practice, I asked two students to interview me about growing up in the Bronx. One student asked me what I did when I was young, and I answered, "Play and go to school." The other then asked, "Did you enjoy growing up? " and my answer was "Sometimes." Then, complete silence. Finally one of the students said, "Thank you," and that was it. The students didn't know how to conduct an interview nor had they taken the time to prepare good interview questions. I suggested we think up questions that dealt in more-detail with growing up and then practice another interview. We simplified Foxfire's "Sample Personality Questions" (see page 121) to come up with the following questions that concentrate on the interviewee's childhood.

1. What was it like when you were young?
2. What games did you play? Who won and lost? How did you feel about winning and losing? Were there ever any fights over games? What were they like?
3. What jokes did you tell?
4. How did your parents treat you?
5. Did you ever have any mystery or adventure when you were a child? What was it?
6. Did you work? What was it like?
7. What did your parents tell you about their parents and grandparents?
8. What do you remember about your grandparents?

We could have made the questionnaire much longer, but I felt the responses to these questions would provide enough information for my

## Practice Interviews
### *Foxfire's "Sample Personality Questions"

1. What were times like when you were a child?
   —How did you and your family live?
   —Were times better, or worse? Why?
   —What is your earliest memory?
2. What types of things did you do as a child?
   —What did you like to do most? Why?
3. How did your parents treat you?
   —What did they do with you that you remember best?
   —What times with them were the most enjoyable to you? Why?
4. What advice or training did your parents give you that has helped you to lead a better, fuller life?
   —What examples did they set for you?
   —How did you profit from them?
   —Do you feel your parents prepared you well for life?
5. As a teenager did your parents let you socialize with boys/girls?
   —Did you have "dates" as we call them now?
   —Where would you go when you went out?
6. What was it like when you first went out on your own?
   —Were times hard?
   —Did you marry?
7. What kind of work did you do to support yourself?
   —Was it difficult?
   —What did it mean to you?
8. How did you feel about living in the country?
   —How about the city?
   —Which do you like best? Why?
9. Do you feel there is a difference between country people and city people?
   —If so, what is it, what makes it so?
10. How big a part has religion played in your life?
    —What are your feelings on it?
    —Do you read the Bible? Should everyone?
    —What is your proof for your belief in God?
    —How has He shown Himself to you?
11. How do you feel about life in general today?
    —How different is it from the way it used to be?
    —Is the quality of life better or worse now?
12. Are people different from what they used to be?
    —In what ways?
    —Are these changes good or bad?
13. How do you feel about the youth of today?
    —Are the teenagers different now, from the way you and your friends are?
    —What has caused these changes?
14. What do you think of the direction our country is going in today?
    —Is American being run well, or badly?
15. What do you consider to be the most valuable possession you have ever had? (Something you *could* not have done without in your lifetime.) Why?
16. Have you done everything in your life you wanted or planned to?
    —If not, what were you not able to do?
17. If you could go back and live your life over, what would you change?
18. How do you feel about:
    —money
    —friendship
    —kindness
    —honesty
19. What do you consider to be vices, or faults, in people?
    —Why are these things bad?
    —How can they be overcome?
20. What advice could you give young people which would help them to lead better lives?
    —What experiences have you had that they could benefit from?

*From *You and Aunt Arie*, Foxfire Foundation, The Foxfire Fund, Inc.

young students to handle. The children practiced some more by interviewing each other. Then we analyzed the interviews. Based on our analysis, I came up with the following do's and don'ts to help students conduct interviews:

1. Avoid yes/no questions. If you do ask them, follow them by asking for an explanation.
2. Pursue an issue.
3. Come back to a question that initially gets you no response—the person you're questioning may not have understood the question.
4. Engage in conversation and don't be afraid to tell a story yourself if you think it will get a response.
5. Encourage people to tell stories, and don't cut them off—be patient and listen carefully.
6. Remember things that you forgot to ask and write them down. You can always do a second interview.
7. The more interested you are in the person you are interviewing the more interesting their stories will be.

**Serendipity**

We discussed one other concept that is crucial for interviewing. It is what Edward Ives, of the University of Maine's North East Archives of Folklore and Oral History, calls serendipity. Serendipity, which means looking for one thing and finding another, has special significance in interviewing. For example, when one boy asked his mother about the games she played, she said she didn't play much. "In fact," she said, "I almost died at eleven." Instead of taking advantage of the serendipity—this interesting unexpected lead—he just went on to the planned question. Serendipity is a component of most really good interviews.

After practicing and analyzing interviews using the questionnaire, we were ready to think about the first formal interviews. At this time the students decided that instead of talking to parents they would interview all the adults at their school—the principal, teachers, aides, food-service workers, secretary and custodians. This plan would make scheduling more manageable, and the students were enthusiastic about the results they might get. We set aside time for students to work on the project for part of two days each week.

Working in the groups of three that would eventually conduct the actual interviews, students practiced using the tape recorder and a quick-developing camera so they could photograph their subjects. Then they made up a large interview-schedule chart and set up appointments with all the adults. At the same time, they asked that interviewees bring pictures of themselves as children.

As the interviews were completed, the students brought them to class and played them for the other students. Everyone had a chance to comment on what parts they thought were particularly interesting, not interesting, or confusing. This gave students a chance to go back and clarify various points with their subjects.

The next step was transcribing. I found that the students needed help. So I sat with them myself as they transcribed or had parent volunteers help. Some groups of students were able to transcribe their own tapes, but others did only a part of theirs with one of the adults finishing it up. After we read and edited the transcripts, we gave them to the interviewees for their approval. We then made any necessary changes. Finally we published our interviews in duplicated booklet form.

### An Unexpected Result

The project lasted almost a semester. Besides all the obvious language benefits, it had one delightful unexpected result. The students began to see the adults around them in a different, more personal, and affectionate light. The fact that all these adults who ran the school had once been children and had the kinds of concerns and problems the students were going through themselves made them more accessible.

Here are some other themes I have found elementary school students like to explore with adults, whether it be in the interviews or simply in discussions:

> What was falling in love like?
> How does it feel to have a baby?
> What travels did you have?
> What is the oldest thing you own and does it have a story?
> Do you still have something you used as a kid? Why did you
> save it? Does it have a story?

I learned one other technique for interviewing at Foxfire that I'm eager to explore; that is to ask someone to take out his or her family photo albums and tell you about the pictures. You could make decent enough copies of the photos with a copier machine and then match the transcribed descriptions of the pictures with the correct photo copies to create a charming anecdotal family history.

# C
# Touching
# Our Educational Past

Some wisdom about teaching from Alice Keliher, whose more than 50 years of experience are an inspiration for those of us who are still struggling to create excellent public schools.

*I*n the course of doing research for a book that deals with the history of conflict over basic skills in American education, I have met and corresponded with many older educators. One person who has been particularly helpful is Alice Keliher, who taught in the 1920s and was Chairperson of the Commission on Human Relations of the Progressive Education Association and professor of education at New York University. I learned (much to my surprise) that in the 1950s Keliher wrote a column quite similar to mine for *Teacher* (then called *Grade Teacher*).

A collection of Keliher's columns was published as *Talks With Teachers* (The Education Publishing Corporation, Darien, Conn., 1958). The forward was written by Eleanor Roosevelt, who spoke directly to teachers: "From the start teachers must realize that they are shaping human beings who must eventually be the kind of people who will be good citizens of a democracy. That was the whole objective of our forefathers in starting public education in our country. They realized that the difficulties of running a democracy could only be met by educated citizens."

Keliher's columns were written during the Cold War period that followed World War II, a time (not unlike ours) when there was a great feeling of uncertainty about the future of the world and a need to reaffirm the values of democracy. These columns provided a reassuring, supportive voice for creative teachers when there were pressures to teach what were called no-frills and no-nonsense basics. She encouraged teachers who wanted to provide their students with opportunities for exploration and decision making.

When I visited Keliher in Peterborough, N.H., she said she thought that the tensions and challenges in the lives of teachers today are similar to those she wrote about and that teachers faced in the 50s and at other times during her sixty-year career.

I think there is much we can learn today from Alice's columns, and I would like to share some of her insights of twenty-five and thirty years ago with you who are teaching today. A central theme that runs through many of Keliher's columns is student and teacher relaxation. In one column she approaches the problem of relaxing during tense times in a delightful, indirect manner:

I would like to see a rocking chair in every classroom, school library, and principal's office. My theory (not proven) is that you cannot stay angry in a rocking chair. The rhythm of rocking has a soothing effect. I am sure that throughout the ages many a troubled person has eased his worries and worked out solutions while rocking . . . look in your attics and barns and see what you have in the way of stowed-away rockers. If you find one, try it at school a few days and see if your tense or troubled children go to it, with or without a book, to enjoy the rhythm and sense of ease. And note whether from time to time you, yourself, breathe a sigh of weariness and take over the rocker.

Now, I do not have a financial interest in furniture companies, but I use the rocking chair as a symbol of what is needed in these troubled times. Life around us is too tense, at times frantic. Tense teachers say and do things in the classroom, or to parents, that they would not if they were relaxed and felt some inner serenity. Tense children and parents say and do things to teachers that they do not mean and later regret. We need to relax, reflect, meditate about how long this old world of ours has been turning in the constellation of planets to orient our little worries.

Keliher has a number of other useful suggestions for easing tension. One point she makes is that teachers have to expect what she calls "unlovable moments." She says that tensions build as expectations of perfection are frustrated. It is crucial to be prepared for conflict, and look at it as part of growth if we are to avoid turmoil and tension within the classroom.

For example, if students pass notes during a reading lesson, or talk when you feel they should be listening, there are nonhostile ways of dealing with the situation. Instead of confiscating the note, you can suggest that notes be passed and read between lessons. Or, if the note is causing no disruption, simply pretend you didn't see it happen. We don't have to consider every little act of secrecy a personal threat to authority and expose it. The same is true of occasional whispering. You can feel more relaxed about it if you remember the times you've whispered in the theater, at a boring lecture, or in the movies. These thoughts can help us stretch the limits of our tolerance and work in a more relaxed environment.

I don't mean to suggest that every inattention or attempt to distract others from listening to what is going on in class should be ignored. As Keliher says in one of her articles, "One can sometimes become more relaxed by expressing anger than by hiding it. Teachers should express anger."

However, anger can be used as theater or as a device rather than a sincere expression of feeling. Not every little attempt at independence or defiance in the classroom merits anger. The genuine expression of anger is much more effective than the use of mock anger (as expressed by raising your voice, or banging a book down on your desk, and so forth). Moreover, the genuine expression of anger is a release of tension, a step towards relaxation. I've found that if I let my students know what makes me angry, and express true anger occasionally, the class becomes more relaxed. The students incorporate the limits of my tolerance into the limits they set for their own behavior in the classroom. Of course, this won't work if you don't give the students some freedom. What you have to do is find the core of your anger and be more tolerant and relaxed about problems around the edges.

Alice Keliher suggests other specific ways of building a relaxed atmosphere in the classroom. She asks, in one article, that teachers think about how much they encourage students to relax during the day. "Are there times that students can express themselves without being judged? Times for them to move and use up accumulated energy?" She feels that physical relaxation is central for mental concentration. I've noticed that youngsters who are full of physical energy cannot relax mentally until they have had a chance to engage in calm, purposeful physical activity. Keliher suggests that dance and expressive movement be integrated into the classroom, and I would add to that noncompetitive games and physical exercise integrated with mime and theater. What Keliher said of children during the 50s is, if anything, more true of children in the 80s:

Today there is much tension among our children. Many have broken families . . . Pressures of other kinds bear down on them. There has probably not been a time when it was so necessary to help children relax, let go, express themselves, feel easy with us and their classmates. Dance and rhythms bring such release. They also provide for creative experience, individual and group.

I'd like to add to Keliher's comment that creative expression is usually confined to the primary grades in school, and that's a pity. The older children get, the more they need to keep on expressing themselves physically as well as mentally. I believe that it would be possible to design research to show that the degree to which the expressive arts are integrated into the curriculum of the upper grades is a good measure of the intensity of discipline problems one will have with the students: the more expressive arts, the fewer the problems.

I'd like to share one other suggestion mentioned in *Talks With Teachers*. In an article called "Teaching Music and Rhythms" Keliher encourages teachers to "fill the day with music." This is above and beyond teaching students to love and perform music. Keliher describes what she means vividly, "In radio and television scripts they use the instruction, 'Bridge With Music,' meaning fill in here while the scene and action are changing. I wish that the children's school day could have many musical bridges with the program flowing from one activity to the next. . . . It hurts to see so many classrooms in which music is relegated to the fixed music period."

Music can put depth and spirit and pleasure into a day. Music during lunch, quiet music during reading time, dance music as an option during recess, music during cleanup are all ways of quietly enriching the life within the classroom and developing a relaxed environment for learning. This is even true if the music is not always calm or slow moving. The wildest rock can have its moment and be a source of relaxation just as a string quartet can. By allowing all sorts of music into the classroom we also help our students come to a complex appreciation of the music of the world instead of limiting their listening.

Reading and writing about Alice Keliher's work has taught me a great deal that I will use in my own work with children. The same is true for other encounters I have had with our educational past. Generally, I've realized how rich our past tradition of open and progressive education is. Past practice can teach a great deal as we try to meet the needs of our students during the next decade. We can learn more from good past practice than from the newest theory or technique that pretends to solve all educational problems.

# D
# *Living Ecology*

A series of suggestions on how to begin environmental sanity in the classroom and the home, and on how to conserve resources and recycle waste.

*H*ave you ever noticed that when you repeat a word over and over and over it begins to lose its meaning? This phenomenon, called verbal satiation by psychologists, frequently comes to my mind during abstract discussions. I remember when I was a graduate student in philosophy, we used to spend hours talking about freedom and will until the very words "freedom" and "will" lost all meaning. The sound of them felt funny on our tongues.

I find the same thing happening to me in discussions about education. Words like "replicable," "cognitive," "affective," "evaluation," and so forth, lose all meaning after a while.

I have found a way to get myself out of this verbal labyrinth, one that might be useful to other teachers. I refer to *Origins* (Macmillan), Eric Partridge's etymological dictionary of the English language. Every time a word confounds me I try to get back to its original meaning and start afresh with some sense of why people began to use the word.

For example, one of the words that has confounded me recently is "scientific." People are always talking about the relevance of social science to education and about the need to make educational experiments more scientific. Yet I have no clear conception of what this means other than that some people would like to apply some of the methods of statistical analysis, a very limited branch of applied mathematics, to some work done in schools.

I went to my Partridge and looked for the root meanings of "science." "Science," as it turns out, comes from the same Indo-European root as the word "scimitar" (the Iranian for knife is scian, and the Sanskrit chjati means, "he cuts"). This root has the general meaning "to cut through" or to get to the core. In this context, science is the pursuit of the relevant, the piercing through unnecessary entanglements to the center of a problem. The original meaning of the word refers to a form of inquiry and not a form of measurement. Many of the things we are doing in schools which cannot be quantified and yet are devoted to getting to the heart of the problem of learning are as scientific in this sense as some sophisticated and yet irrelevant form of measurement.

## Household Wisdom

There is another popular word whose meaning is sometimes lost in the flow of argument. That word is "ecology." The root of the word is "eco" which has its origins in the Greek "oikos" which means house or household. "Logy," which comes from the Greek "logos," means the word or wisdom about some subject. Ecology, then, is wisdom about the household. Recently the word "ecology" has come to be extended to refer to the whole environment in which life exists. In this sense, ecology is the wisdom we can master about the earth household; it is a consisderation of the whole earth as a house which we must care for since it is our place of dwelling.

We have not been very wise with respect to the care of our earth household. Man produces more than he consumes and accumulates waste products that poison his environment and which may eventually destroy life.

The classroom is an ideal place for the young to begin to learn about the care of the environment. It is possible to study ecology in a formal way. It is also possible to live it.

One way to begin is to survey the waste that accumulates in the classroom during the course of a day or week and see how much of it can be used instead of dumped.

In the classroom there are usually a number of organic waste products such as chewing gum, candy, banana peels, apple rinds, and bread crumbs. These products are usually dumped into the same can as nonorganic wastes like paper, old pencils, plastic pens, used notebooks, and so forth. Yet these two categories of waste products cannot be disposed of in the same way. The organic waste, in fact, can be used very profitably if one has a small gardening plot in the school, for they can be used to create a compost heap that will develop fertilizer for the garden. In fact, two waste baskets—one marked organic and one nonorganic—can be the beginning of wise housekeeping in the classroom.

There is a lot that can be done with nonorganic waste. Old papers can be used to make papier maché or can be worked into collages and paintings. They can be used as note scraps, as towels, as wrappings for packages. Pencil stubs can be broken apart and the wood used in small constructions while the lead can be accumulated and used in mechanical pencils. The parts of plastic pens can also be used in many ways. The springs can be used for scientific experimentation, the cartridges for collages and constructions that can decorate the room. I have seen, for example, a wall constructed out of old ball-point pens glued together.

The wall is constantly added to as new waste develops and is very functional in the classroom as a divider to make private spaces.

One need not confine the class to studying ways of using waste products in the classroom alone. In our school we have a class in automotive mechanics. The class has spent a lot of time going to junkyards and empty lots where the students have found old engines and carburetors and gear boxes. They have learned to make discarded parts clean and functional. They have also learned how to make their own tools out of discarded scraps of metal and wood. With a soldering iron, a hack saw and a few other tools, students can make hammers, screwdrivers, drills, and so forth. In this way, they can see the transformation of waste products into useful objects.

### Useful Waste

There are a lot of other wastes that can be collected and reused in the schools. Old clothes can be used for costumes, or remade into new clothes. Advertisements, old posters and discarded billboard sections make wonderful reading material and decorations. Last year I found a "sign graveyard" near our school. A large lot was filled with old signs. There were ten-foot-tall letters, large soda bottles and such. We asked for some of the signs for our school and were given them. The letters and figures were worked into a fantasy playground. Other letters and figures were taken apart and the wood and metal were used for other purposes.

We found that mattress factories have more scraps than they can sensibly dispose of, and so we used them to stuff pillows and cushions, to make stuffed animals and to weave large tapestries.

In a modest way students can help to develop ways of managing our earth household more wisely. They can be told about the interrelationships of various forms of life and can study life systems. But they can also begin to act upon their own to waste less and want less. They can use their ingenuity in developing new uses for old things and find ways of making our environment less cluttered. Perhaps they can even influence their parents to care more about the way in which they use or discard objects.

However, it is not enough to look at our immediate environment as we are part of an earth system in which events all over the globe influence each other. The recent energy crises are dramatic though not unique instances of interaction on an earthwide scale. I've found that young people's understanding of events such as these are minimal and I worry about the implications of global ignorance for our ability to create a sane earth environment. For example, I asked a group of fourth-, fifth-, and sixth-grade students what the energy crisis was all about and got the following answers: "It's when the Arabs won't give us oil," "It's when they raise prices so you can't get the gas," "It's when you use up too much energy so there isn't enough for everybody," "It's when there are too many cars and not enough gas."

Like many adults, the children were aware that there are currently many problems concerning energy and that the interrelationships of cars, money, gas, and some foreign nations are involved. However, also like many adults, they had no coherent picture of the way oil is acquired, used, and paid for in our society. In fact they had little understanding of energy, its manifestations, and purposes.

Since all of our lives are and will continue to be affected by the use people make of energy resources, it seems crucial to me to discuss the subject in the classroom even though the related issues surrounding it are complex. I wanted to give my students as much of an understanding of the ways energy can be developed and controlled as possible. Because of this concern I developed an energy curriculum.

## The Essence of Energy

The curriculum begins with a consideration of energy itself. The introduction demonstrates the role that energy plays in animating an inert system. When I tested the curriculum I began by putting five billiard balls in a wooden box (about 2 feet by 3 feet). With the balls completely still, the children and I considered the following question: How can we make the balls move? That one simple question actually generated a number of various "right" answers: "By hitting the balls with a stick," "by pushing the balls with your hands," "by lifting and tipping the box," "by pumping strong blasts of air at the balls," "by moving the table the box is on." We realized that each of these techniques depended on energy provided by human motion. Hand pushing required a direct infusion of energy, but in the case of the stick and the blasts of air a separate vehicle was used to transmit the energy to the balls. When we tipped the box and moved the table, energy was applied to the whole system (box and balls together) and the movement of the box caused the balls to move.

After playing with the box for awhile we considered two additional questions: What happens when you stop putting energy into the system? What other everyday items needed energy in order to work? It became clear to the students that you had to keep putting energy into any process or system to keep it working. One student immediately realized the connection between what we'd been discussing and the use of gas by cars. She saw the car as an inert system that needs an infusion of energy in order to work. The problem with systems that need energy, one student commented, is that "they're hungry all the time."

### Those Gas Guzzlers

To capitalize on our discussion about how hungry cars are, I suggested we try to figure out how big a tank we'd need to travel across the country without stopping for gas. We estimated that the trip from San Francisco to New York is 2,500 miles and that our car gets 20 miles to the gallon, therefore, the trip would require 125 gallons. Since a one-gallon can is about 10 inches high by 6 inches long by 4 inches wide, we figured that if we put the 125 gallons in one-gallon cans and stretched these out, they would span a distance of 1,250 inches (10 inches by 125) long, or about 104 feet. If piled up, the tank might be represented by a five-can cubic rectangle (5 by 5 by 5) or a rectangular gas tank about 6 feet by 2½ feet by 1⅔ feet.

As we were doing all that calculating it occurred to me that the students were using most of their mathematical skills without thinking about them at all. So I decided to continue in this direction. As a homework assignment, I had the students ask their parents to estimate how many miles they drove in a year and the number of miles they got to the gallon. The students were to figure out the size tank it would take to hold the gas they used for a year's driving. I told the students that they could help each other with the calculations so that no one would be penalized for not being proficient in math.

When we got our results, everyone realized the staggering amount of gasoline used just by the parents of one group of students in one year. One student speculated that the tank needed to hold all the gas used for one car over a 100-year period might even be larger than the earth itself.

We went on to consider other systems that need infusions of energy like wind-up toys, clocks, radios, electric lights, ovens, heaters, and even people. This led us to consider energy conversion. We talked about how the energy derived from food in one form converts to another form to enable us to move and think. Another example of energy conversion is the way in which a battery chemically stores energy and then releases it in the form of electricity to power something such as the motion of some of the battery-operated toys we studied.

**The Sun**

Finally we looked at the most dramatic and omnipresent source of energy—the sun. Most of my students' families have gardens, and the children have seen the transformation of seeds into flowers, fruits and vegetables, even considering how plant growth is stimulated by energy from the sun. This summer I watched corn grow for the first time and began to realize how early people could believe there was something divine about the plant itself and the sun that gave it energy.

The students also experimented with other practical uses of solar energy. They magnified the sun's rays to set fires. We use a simple box lined with aluminum foil to set up a solar cooker. A final experiment involved solar heat. We cut holes in the top of a small wooden box lined with insulation material and fitted metal cans into them. After filling the cans with water, we put the box directly into the sun. When the water in the cans heated up, it warmed the box. We found that on a sunny day the water would heat up enough to keep the box warm through the night.

(For a packet containing experiments with solar energy write to Bay Area Energy Action Center, Fort Mason Center, San Francisco, CA 94123. The packet is free, but $2 is required to cover first-class postage.)

**Energy and Politics**

After considering energy from a scientific point of view, and beginning to understand its various sources, we began to look at the social implications of control of energy. The students wondered why there's such an obsession with gasoline and other oil products while solar energy seems to be under utilized. I suggested that the students do some research on who owns the oil companies, on how much money they earn, on why there are so many cars, on the history of the development of solar power, hydroelectric power, and so forth. To keep from getting bogged down in the complexities of the energy situation each student took one energy-related, social problem to research. Some of the topics were:

How much work and money are being invested in developing solar energy?

How much profit did the oil companies make last year, and how does that compare with profits of other kinds of companies?

What do the oil companies say about the oil crisis?
What do environmentalists say about the oil crisis?
Where are the main sources of oil in the world and who con-
trols them?
Have any groups of companies or governmental bodies begun
to plan new ways to use energy? To deal with transporta-
tion? To provide energy for factories?
Do all countries use the same amount of energy per person?
Have any countries developed ways to cut down on oil use?

In order to get some answers to these complex questions I suggested
that the students write to some of the following sources asking specific
questions about oil and the energy crisis:

The oil companies—to request their annual reports and any
literature they might have published on the oil crisis
The Environmental Protection Agency—for reports of the ef-
fects of oil development on the environment
The U. S. Energy Department—for documents on research
projects in alternative energy development
The Council on Environmental Quality of the Executive
Office of the President
The energy departments of various states, especially in the
Gulf Coast and the West where there has been considerable
oil development
GOO (Get Oil Out), Santa Barbara, CA 93102
Friends of the Coast, Box 583, Bodega Bay, CA 94923
The Sierra Club, 530 Bush Street, San Francisco, CA 94108
University of California Appropriate Technology Program,
4455 Chemistry Annex, University of California, Davis,
CA 95616

In addition these sources I suggested that students keep a dated file of
newspaper clippings relating to energy, and that they pay as much
attention to the business pages of the newspapers as to the headlines.
Obviously this is a long-term project and I hope that some of my students
will continue on their own. It is particularly important for us here in
Point Arena, CA, where the community is currently involved in a
struggle over whether or not to support local oil development. But it is
vitally important for all of us to be informed about this issue since the
future will be determined to some great degree by what we do about
energy today. Though I have my own opinions about oil development

and the control of energy resources, I do not want to propagandize my students. What I am hoping to do is to help them—over a period of time—with the research skills and information that will enable them to make intelligent decisions about energy concerns as well as other important issues.

## Postscript

I received a letter complaining about my views on the energy curriculum and believe it's worth sharing that letter as well as my response:

I have just read Herb Kohl's article, "An energy curriculum" . . . When he closes by saying that he does not wish to propagandize his students, I am astonished, for in his *choice* of questions to be answered by the students, he has clearly biased their research. At the risk of being thought an apologist for the oil companies, I will say that I am certain their rate of profit has little if anything to do with the energy problem. *If* they are making too much profit, then the price of oil products is too high to us—which is logically unrelated to the worldwide shortage. Further, most of the organizations he lists as information sources already have positions on the issues which amount to one side. I believe all are anti-nuclear, for example. I see none that are pro-coal. And so on. I hope you will seek someone to write a more balanced article, naming sources which have different points of view. This article surprises me all the more in that in the past I have found *Teacher* a very objective periodical.

Rinehart S. Potts
Assistant Professor
Glassboro State College
Glassboro, New Jersey

### My response

Professor Potts must surely realize that questions can have many different answers. I did not set up rhetorical questions but did open up some issues that are not usually asked. As for sources, one of the first I recommended was corporate reports, straight from the horse's mouth, you might say.

I do believe that profits have something to do with the manipulation of energy resources, that all that issues from the oil companies is not neutral, and that solar and other nonpolluting energy sources are our best hopes for survival. In that the professor is right that I have opinions. Nevertheless I did not write advocating one way of looking at the energy problem so much as suggesting that there might be more than one way to look at it.

# E
# Inflation,
# Self-Sufficiency,
# and Small-Scale Economics

This is an attempt to help students analyze their needs and design sensible economic programs using the resources they are likely to have available in their lives. Its premise is that people must learn how to share the resources of the planet.

*I*nflation, the rise of prices beyond what many people can afford, has a major effect upon children's lives as well as upon the lives of their parents. It's easy to forget that students are also affected by inflation and are often confused because so many problems in their lives are attributed to it.

Recently, I discussed the subject of inflation with a group of fourth, fifth, and sixth graders. I found that all the students were worried because they often heard their parents complain about high prices and paying their bills, and worrying about what will happen over the next few years. The students made it clear that they wanted to know what they could do about this inflation they kept hearing about but didn't really understand. In response, I decided to dramatize the cumulative effects of inflation over six years and then to introduce the topic of self-sufficiency, which can help alleviate the problem.

### Dollar Help

We began by assuming that, for each of the six years, each student would be alloted $100. This money would be used for helping parents, personal spending and savings. At the beginning of the first year, we all had our money allocated in the same way:

| | |
|---|---:|
| Help with rent | $20 |
| Help with food | 20 |
| Help with taxes | 15 |
| Some of our clothes | 15 |
| Movies, etc. | 15 |
| Save | 15 |
| Total | $100 |

Next, I explained to the group that prices in the United States were rising by about 13 percent a year. We figured this meant that what we could buy with $100 at the beginning of the year would cost 13 percent more, or $113, by the end. We looked at it another way, too: At the end of one year of 13 percent inflation, our $100 would buy only about $87 worth of goods. The students realized that the only way to "keep up" would be to make more and more money each year, and that most workers don't get 13 percent raises.

I gave each student a copy of the chart shown below to use to allocate his or her shrinking money over the six years.

To calculate the increase in prices under an inflation rate of 13 percent beginning with $100, I used this simple formula:

Year 1: $100
Year 2: $100 + $13 (13 percent of $100) = $113
Year 3: $113 + $14.69 (13 percent of $113) = $127.69
Year 4: $127.69 + $16.59 (13 percent of $127.69) =$144.28.

|  | Year 1 | Year 2 | Year 3 | Year 4 | Year 5 | Year 6 |
|---|---|---|---|---|---|---|
| Money to spend (at 13% inflation) | $100 | $87 | $72 | $55 | $37 | $16 |
| Help with rent | 20 | | | | | |
| Help with food | 20 | | | | | |
| Help with taxes | 15 | | | | | |
| Own clothes | 15 | | | | | |
| Entertainment | 15 | | | | | |
| Save | 15 | | | | | |
| What things cost (another way of looking at the same problem) | $100 | $113 | $128 | $145 | $163 | $184 |

I rounded off the figures to the nearest dollar. To arrive at the figures for the amount of money (in terms of "Year 1" dollars) that the children will have to spend each year, I subtracted the amount of increased cost due to inflation from what had been available to spend in the previous year.

"Year 2" was a problem for all of us since we all had the same expenses, but the same items would now cost $113. In essence our $100 had shrunk to $87 in value. We would have to give up something and we each found different ways of dealing with that first year of inflation. Some students cut down on their own clothes, entertainment, and savings in order to keep their contributions to the family at the same level. Others cut proportionally and spent a little less on everything. We also discussed the issue of whether taxes and rent would remain constant or rise.

"Year 3" became a much greater problem, and by the time the students reached "Year 4," they realized that they had the same expenses and about half as much to spend. One student said that "Year 3" ought to be called "the inflation year," because that's when you realize that there really is trouble.

By "Year 6" students were talking about ways of earning extra money, moving to cheaper places to live, growing their own food, making their own clothes, and moving in with friends and relatives. On their own, they had introduced the issue of self-sufficiency and identified it as a necessity during a long period of inflation.


### Simplifying


At first we considered self-sufficiency on an individual basis: What can an individual do for himself or herself that can make life simpler and less dependent upon money? We took all of the categories in the chart and considered this question: What can I do to make myself more self-sufficient with regard to:

*Rent or a place to live?*   Students didn't have many suggestions. Some suggested learning how to use tools and how to fix electrical appliances, plumbing, and so on. I suggested that students ask their parents how much they paid other people to fix things around their homes. We came up with figures ranging from nothing to several hundred dollars.

Both parents of the child who reported no expenses were carpenters and had taught themselves how to do all their own home repairs. I invited them to come to class and describe how they had developed their skills. As a result, I've resolved to develop curriculum materials on home repair for elementary school students.

*Food?*   Most students saw that they could grow a lot of their own food if they just tried. We examined the possibility of gardening in an apartment or on a small plot in a city and found that, with care, a considerable part of one's produce can be grown in even the most unlikely of urban conditions. The book *My Garden Companion: A Complete Guide for the Beginner* by Jamie Jobb (Sierra Club/Scribner's) was one helpful resource.

*Taxes?*   Students agreed that there is no way around paying taxes, and that they would help, like it or not. Our discussion of taxes led to a consideration of Proposition 13, the property tax limitation in California. One student asked what taxes were used for anyway, and I got one chart showing how federal taxes were spent and another showing the allocation of state and local funds.

*Clothes?*   Many students were already learning to make clothes for themselves. This was especially true of the girls. In fact, when one boy said that it would be impossible for him to make his own clothes, a girl responded sarcastically, "As impossible as for me to fix a leak in the roof or change a tire." This led to a heated discussion of sex stereotypes. It was interesting to see the boys so defensive. Most such discussions have to do with what girls can't do, but here were the boys defending their inability to make clothes. Out of the talk came the decision to start a mixed sewing group in which the girls would teach the boys how to make fancy disco shirts. It seemed the disco theme would help the boys save face.

*Entertainment?*   The students knew all the eonomic facts of life on this subject. Concerts and movies were getting more and more expensive. The price of candy in the movies had tripled over the past few years, so that a number of students were taking their own snacks.

One girl commented that she used to go to the movies every week, but that now she and her friends go about once a month. She said that on other weekends they get together and put on their own discos and shows. There was a general consensus that entertainment is hard to provide by yourself, but with a few friends you can make do.

Students talked about the idea of pooling money to buy and share records and books. In this context I mentioned the food club my family belongs to. Each of the twelve families that belongs takes a turn running the club once a year. That family orders the food for a month in bulk, picks it up and sets up a time for the other families to pick up their orders. The club also keeps a store of staples such as peanut butter, oil, honey, pasta, and rice. The store stays with the family who is buying for the month and all the families can buy staples from it at any time. By buying wisely and in bulk we have been able to cut down on the cost of items available to us by approximately one third.

The reason I spent so much time describing the food club was that I wanted to point out that self-sufficiency need not be limited to individuals. Often a small group can provide for itself in a more effective way than can either an individual or the larger society. Food clubs are just one kind of organizing that E. F. Schumacher talks about in his book *Small is Beautiful: Economics as if People Mattered* (Harper & Row). Small groups of people working together can often provide a sensible self-sufficient alternative to dependence upon large bureaucracies, and can work as a hedge against the problems of inflation. The ways in which my students solved their entertainment problems are good examples of collective self-sufficiency. Other examples are neighborhood gardens, exchanges of services instead of money, and cooperative baby-sitting arrangements. All of these forms of barter are ironically more sensible that the more modern form of exchanging money for goods and services in times of extreme inflation.

*Savings?*   Is it possible to save anything during times of inflation? Is it worth it, since what you save decreases in value over a period of time? I told my students that I have no answers to those questions, and that the problem of saving at least a little when expenses keep getting harder to cover is one that bothers me all the time.

I told the group that no matter what the situation, I try to put a little money away each time I get some, and pretend I never received it. It's almost as if I have to deceive myself into saving a little for the sake of a very uncertain future. I shared with my students my own feeling that we all have to do something that shows that, no matter how difficult things appear now, we still believe in the future.

Self-sufficiency led to a more general discussion of work and money. There are many ways of dealing with work and money in the classroom. One way is to invite people from many walks of life to talk to the children about their work. Another way is to have them read about and see films about work and to study together qualifications and general pay scales for various jobs. A third way, the one I've concentrated on is to set up small, cooperatively run student businesses in a classroom or school. As well as raising money for class projects, the process helps to integrate a sense of self-sufficiency into the students' everyday lives.

Operating a real business in their classroom or school gives kids the chance to have meaningful experiences with the business end of things as well as with buying and selling. No matter how enthusiastic students are about starting a business of their own (and they usually jump at the chance) they immediately have to face the reality of a need for resources to capitalize their business. For example, a group of my students listed the following types of businesses they would like to operate: a toy store, a book store, a theater, a repair shop, a newspaper, a food store, and a movie-making and picture-taking company.

After listing all of these possibilities the students and I discussed which businesses we could start with the resources already available to us and which would require some start-up money. We began with the toy store. At first the students said they wanted to buy all new toys and then resell them. However, they quickly realized that if a toy cost them $4 in a local store and they tried to sell it for $5, no one would buy it from *them*.

When one student then asked how stores got their toys, I introduced the notion of wholesale as opposed to retail purchasing. Realizing that we had no money to buy lots of toys wholesale, the students became discouraged. I promised to invite a wholesaler to school to explain how it might be possible to buy items wholesale or at discounts of up to 50 percent.

At that point we started to do a little arithmetic. I asked how much money could be made on 20 $4 toys that we bought at a 50 percent discount and sold for $4. The group worked out the problem: 20 toys at $4 each means we would have to pay out $80, if we bought the toys retail. At a 50 percent discount we would actually have to pay $40 and could make $40 for the class. However, as one student pointed out, we would have to sell all of the toys we bought to make that much and at least eleven toys to make any profit. Therefore, another added, we'd have to be really careful about picking a toy that would be popular—or we might even lose money.

After that discussion I based a number of math problems that dealt with finding profit, loss, and so forth, on figures from a chart with columns to include: "Retail Price," "Discount," "Wholesale Price," "Amount Made on Each Item," "Number Bought," "Number Sold," "Profit or Loss." For some problems I gave the students the retail price, the discount and the number of items bought and sold and asked them to figure out the rest. Later I left other unknowns.

This group had already had some experience with percentages. With a younger group I would have simplified the columns on the chart to read: "Retail," "Wholesale," "Amount We Make for Each One Sold," "Number Bought," "Number Sold," "Profit or Loss."

Several days later we came back to the question of opening a store. We had no capital, but one student suggested that the children could donate books, toys and comics that they didn't want and have a store that sold used things instead of new ones.

Another child said that when he had told his mother about the idea of having a store in the class, she had suggested that the students make stationery and greeting cards to sell to other children and people in the community. The students agreed to begin with both suggestions. There was material already in their classroom to make woodblock designs and print stationery. And they had books and toys they were willing to donate. I said that I would donate a small printing set (the kind you can get in a stationery store that is used to make stamps of addresses and names) and suggested that the students could also personalize stationery.

Once a decent number of toys, books, comics and packages of stationery had accumulated, we had the problem of how to keep track. Solving it led to helping the students set up the "books" for their business. These included "In Stock" and "Sold" files and sales, expense and balance sheets. Any kind of student-run, money-making enterprise can be operated under the system.

After I explained the word *inventory*, we wrote up a three-by-five index card for each item we planned to sell. Each card gave the nature of the item (Wonder Woman comic), the cost to our class ($0.00) and the sale price ($0.10). Next we labeled two file boxes—one "In Stock" and the other "Sold." When an item was sold, the card was to be taken from the "In Stock" box and put in the "Sold" box. In that way the students would always know what they had sold and what was left (discounting thefts, which are always a possibility in any store, including those run by students).

We set up the sales sheet so that the salesperson on duty could keep a record of every purchase made at the store. It, too, was in chart form, including the following columns across the top: "Item Sold," "Number Sold," "Date Sold," "Salesperson," "Price Received." At the bottom of the page we included a row for tallying the total sales in number of items and total money collected for that sheet.

We used the expense sheet to account for any expenses incurred in the operation of the store and included these headings: "Expense Item," "Number Bought," "Date," "Purchaser," "Amount Paid." At the bottom of this page, too, we left room for a tallying row.

At the end of each week I insisted that the students tally expenses and sales and record them on the balance sheet, which we columned this way: "Week of ____/____ to ____/____," "Amount Earned," "Expenses," "Amount Earned After Expenses," "Previous Balance," "Total."

At first a few students felt that all this record-keeping was a lot of work for a little store. But as sales began to grow and students began to want to develop new projects with their profits they understood the reason for putting down so many numbers.

The student store needn't become a highly competitive place where students fight over who sells the most and who gets the profits. I have found that such activities can just as easily foster cooperation and a feeling of doing things for the group. It all depends on the spirit with which the business is created and the fairness with which the money is put to use.

Here are a few money-making projects that don't take too much capitalization and can be exciting learning experiences.

> A theater group that charges a small fee for plays put on after school and in the evening. (I don't think in-school plays and activities should be charged for.)
>
> A student-run classified ad newspaper in which students who want jobs or can provide services (such as repairing bicycles) or want to buy or sell things can advertise. Ads can cost about 20 cents, and the paper can sell for 10 cents. It might include some short articles and puzzles and cartoons as well as ads.
>
> A photography studio run by student photographers with the help of some faculty or community member. I have always wondered if it wouldn't work to have the students take their own class photos and use the money they make on school-related projects.
>
> A repair shop for fixing skates, bikes, toys, furniture, and so forth.
>
> A more ambitious project would be a natural food store and garden. Students could grow spices; plant and can vegetables; grow fruit trees; or buy fruit and make jams, jellies, and preserves or any combination of these. With careful planning such gardening could even be done inside or in wooden boxes on roofs and balconies of urban schools. You would need a highly fertilized soil and some greenhouse structure to protect against frost. There are many excellent gardening books to consult. One good one on indoor gardening is *Crockett's Book of Indoor Gardening* (Little, Brown).

# IV
# Helping Students Think, Respond, and Learn

# A
# Learning About Learning and Looking

How an explicit study of techniques of learning
and observation can help students.

*B*y studying and thinking about how learning happens, students can strengthen their own learning skills. It's possible to use the learning process as a curriculum theme on almost any grade level. For example, I recently asked a group of third and fourth graders: "Do you remember how you learned anything?"

One boy said that he remembered learning how to ride a two-wheel bike. He said that he was afraid to fall and so before he tried riding he watched his big sister and her friends ride. Before he went to sleep at night he visualized how he'd get on the bike and imagined himself riding. After awhile he had practiced so much in his mind that he felt ready. Then he just went out and rode the bike. He said he learned to ride in his mind.

Another student also remembered learning to ride a bike, but it happened to her in a different way. She wasn't afraid to fall, and she tried and tried, falling a lot, until she learned to keep her balance and ride without falling.

### No One Way to Learn

Other students remembered how they learned to swim, to write their names, to play games or sing a song. One boy said that he learned to swim by kicking and moving his arms while a grownup held him up in the water. Another student said that he learned to play checkers by asking his aunt to show him the moves. As the students spoke about the ways they had learned I jotted down notes. What emerged from our discussion was the idea that there isn't just one way to learn how to ride a bike or swim or to do any of the things mentioned. Moreover, it became clear that there isn't any one approach to learning for each student. For example, one child asked about and learned the rules of a game in advance but plunged in and made mistakes with a bike; for another child the pattern was reversed. The students realized that each of them learned differently under different circumstances.

**Ways to Learn**

To conclude our discussion we made a list of the different ways of learning that had come up:

1. Learning by watching
2. Learning by practicing in your imagination
3. Learning by trying to do something right away and not worrying about making mistakes
4. Learning by letting someone help you and do part of it for you
5. Learning by asking questions.

After putting this list on the chalkboard, for homework I asked the students to find someone else—a friend, maybe a baby or a grownup who was learning something new—and observe how he or she was going about it. I encouraged them to ask the learners they chose some questions about what they were experiencing.

Several days later I asked the children what subjects they had chosen for observation and what they had seen. One student had watched his older sister in the process of learning to drive; another had watched his baby brother, who was learning to walk. Other observations included learning to use a tape recorder, learning to play a new song on the piano, learning to talk, learning a new (second) language, learning to cook a new recipe, learning to use public transportation, learning to open a savings account and learning to build a bookcase.

To help the students articulate what they had observed I put a chart with the following headings on the chalkboard: "What Is Being Learned," "Who Is Learning," "Who or What Is Helping," "What the Learner Is Doing," "Problems in Learning," "How the Learner Felt."

The student who had watched his sister learn to drive volunteered to describe what he had observed. He said his sister had used a driver's handbook and also had been helped by their parents. First she had read the book and then gone driving with her mother.

When her brother quizzed her about her learning she told him that she imagined driving all the time and felt that she got as much practice in her head as in the car. She also explained that she practiced in the family car when it was in the garage, trying to feel comfortable with the wheel and pedals. She said her main problem was getting used to all the other cars on the road when she was still learning to control her car. Since she sometimes felt there were too many things to worry about at one time, she and her parents decided she could simplify the task by practicing on a back road where there was little traffic.

She told him, too, that the whole idea of learning to drive made her very nervous. She was afraid of failing her driver's test and imagined her friends making fun of her. She said this anxiety sometimes came to her mind as she practiced driving and messed up her learning.

### Classroom Learning

Another student raised his hand at this point and said that he had the same trouble with reading lessons in school. He said he felt so nervous when other students were around that he couldn't concentrate on the page. This student's comments gave me an idea for taking the students' thinking a step further. I suggested that they use the points we'd been discussing to analyze their own ways of learning in school.

I hoped this exercise would give them a technique for understanding their learning problems, finding alternative approaches and thus taking control of their own learning. Maybe the boy who was anxious about reading needed to simplify things by reading when other people weren't around. Or, perhaps he could try a different way to learn to read, such as not thinking about being right all the time and not worrying excessively about mistakes. I've seen many students get trapped into making the same mistakes over and over because they can't change habits that get in the way of learning. They are unaware of the variety of strategies that are available to someone trying to learn something new.

The students' analyses of their own learning in the classroom amazed me. I got more insights into the children's feelings about school and needs from discussions of these thoughts during the following week than I'd been able to gather over the previous few months. I realized that some students who seemed uninterested in reading were actually learning by watching other students. Others, who made a lot of mistakes, were learning by plunging in and not being afraid to take their falls. A few students were able to articulate for the first time the paralyzing effect that anxiety about other students' opinions of them had on their reading or math performances.

### Profiles of Learning

As a final exercise with this group I suggested each child do a profile of the way he or she usually learns. I wanted to help the students pin down concretely what they had found out about themselves as learners so that they could shift techniques if they were getting stuck, frustrated or paralyzed by anxiety.

The profile was very simple. Each student had a hypothetical 100 learning points to distribute over the five learning techniques we'd come up with earlier: 1. Watching; 2. Practicing in imagination; 3. Doing and not worrying about mistakes; 4. Having someone do part of it for you; 5. Asking questions. I duplicated a graph (an example of which is shown below) for each child, and each distributed the 100 points according to his or her analysis of personal learning style.

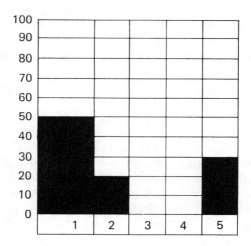

I make it clear to the students that no one technique was better than another, that there might be techniques that we hadn't thought of and finally, that personal profiles change over time and when different types of things have to be learned.

I intend to use the same method of analyzing learning the fifth and sixth graders during the next few months. And I've decided to add another component to the study of learning—the study of how animals learn and experience the world.

I hoped that by observing animals students would develop the patience to observe human behavior as well and develop the habit of thinking about what they experienced of the world.

There are a number of ways to observe animal behavior and it is useful to begin a study of animal behavior by discussing modes of observation. One way to begin is by imagining what it would be like to study the behavior of animals by watching them in a zoo. The big cats pace back and forth endlessly; the birds of prey sit chained to trees; the alligators and turtles lie dormant in a small pool of water surrounded by a fence. The zoo is an environment that modifies their behavior. They cannot be natural in unnatural circumstances. Yet most of the science that is taught in school involves the manipulation of things in unnatural settings. We have to learn how to let things be, how to understand and respect things in their natural environments without destroying them.

One way to begin is by learning how to observe some living thing without trying to control it or interfere in its life.

Think of an insect that lives in your environment; say an ant. How could you and your students learn about its life? One way would be to capture it and watch how it functions in a jar. But this would be a bad choice because an ant cannot live and perform its ordinary life functions without being part of a community.

### Concentration

Another way would be to look at one ant, but this is not as easy as it sounds. To follow a single ant with your eyes and not lose it under a leaf or confuse it with other ants takes intense concentration. I have tried myself, first for a few seconds at a time, then gradually building up to five or ten minutes. I've tried the same thing with my first graders. At first they thought the whole idea was a joke. Then they began to realize how tired you can get by simply watching. We all had to learn how to slow down, quiet down and keep from being distracted. It was almost a form of meditation.

After following a single ant, the class decided to map the distance one travelled. We drew pictures of its trail and noted each time it stopped to pick up a piece of food or to fight or to help another ant. Then I asked the children if they thought all ants were alike. How can you tell ants apart without marking them?

This train of thought involved us in a different kind of observation, since we were now considering physical appearance and temperment rather than movement. Some ants were small; others very large. One student noticed that some of the ants had broken limbs or antennae; another observed that certain ones moved faster than others and always seemed to be fighting.

We could have gone from the observation of ants into an analysis of the structure of ant communities and the anatomy of ants. However, the phenomenon of observing seemed more interesting, so I introduced the class to Jakob von Uexkull's essay "A Stroll Through the World's of Animals and Men: A Picture Book of Invisible Worlds" (reprinted in *Instinctive Behavior*, ed. Claire H. Schiller, International Universities Press, New York, 1957). This essay includes a series of pictures of an oak tree viewed from the perspective of many different creatures. The pictures show the tree as perceived by a woodsman, a scared little child, a fox, an owl, an ant, a bark beetle and an ichneumon fly. In each case the tree is perceived and experienced in a different manner. I asked the class to think of what a tree means to an animal that lives in its roots as opposed to one that lives in its branches, to think of the size of the tree from the ant's perspective and to think of the tree's magical powers as projected by the scared child.

At this point we shifted our discussion from observing things to trying to understand how others perceive their world. Drawing is a wonderful tool for this. We drew pictures of a person from the perspective of a bird, a dog and a mouse. Then we started looking at each other and talking about the different ways people perceive the world. It was not as much a matter of making a judgment about one person's perception being better than another's as an attempt to recreate the quality and individuality of each other's experiences.

If you are lucky enough to have a camera in your classroom, the differences in perspective can be more dramatically illustrated. One group of students can photograph the class from the floor, while other children can stand on chairs and take pictures of the same people and activities. The developed pictures can be mounted next to each other to display alternate views of the same events.

The book *Cosmic View: The Universe in 40 Jumps* by Kees Boeke (John Day, New York, 1957) will give the same kinds of perspectives. A woman is shown sitting on a chair holding a baby. There is a mosquito on one of her hands. The first picture is taken from about 10 meters above the woman. The second, a drawing, shows the woman from 100 meters above. Each of the next 18 pictures increases the distance from which the woman is seen by the same factor of 10, until the viewer is well into the solar system and galaxy.

After 20 leaps out, the first picture is shown again. Then the drawings move into the woman's hand by a decreasing factor of 10, so that one sees the mosquito in detail and then in the woman's blood stream. The final pictures view the world on an atomic and subatomic level. This is one of the most dramatic illustrations of perceptual relativity I have seen.

If you have no camera, children can look at the same phenomenon in many different ways. This can be done physically, simply by spending an hour on the floor, an hour on a ladder and an hour sitting in a chair. A class can be observed from the front, back, or middle of the room. An activity can be observed from a distance and from close up. It can be studied by listening to other people's descriptions of it.

### How Others See Us

With older children it is possible to pursue actual observations of animals and things further and record them in written form. For example, ask students to walk into a room, observe it closely and then try to determine the kind of person or family that lives there. Another interesting area for observation is the playground. How do different people approach games? Who avoids playing? Who plunges in? What can you learn about learning and about how different beings experience things from simply watching and trying to project yourself into another's world?

Looking is not always neutral. We often see what we want to see, and one of the benefits of observations that are consciously shifted is that we can uncover our own prejudices as well as discover how others see us. I have found it useful to ask myself the following questions: What do I ask of the phenomenon? What do I try to tease out of it? What do I expect from it? What do I wish from it? What about it feels comfortable? What feels uncomfortable about it? What do I like about it? What do I dislike about it?

It is easiest to train one's habits of looking by first observing animals and asking these questions. But the human implications are most important. There is so much racial, sexual, and class intolerance in our society that we have to begin to undo an unlooking way of living with others.

In working with elementary school children attending recently desegregated schools, I have found many are unable to look at each other even on the simple level of exchanging a glance. As a way of helping them see each other as people, I began with animals and with a discussion about "looking." Eventually they began to observe each other and themselves to try to answer the same questions. And in doing so, they began to learn from each other by exchanging perceptions of the world. They also began to take time to think about how others learned and approached problems and broadened their own ways of dealing with new and unfamiliar experiences.

# B
# Some Techniques for Thinking

On showing students the use of imaginative
techniques in problem solving.

*G*iving and getting feedback, creating systems from scratch, turning things upside down, making new combinations, inventing totally new objects and techniques, using negative thinking and ignorance positively—all are ways of enhancing students' problem-solving skills.

## 1. Feedback

The word "feedback" is of recent origin though the idea of feedback is very old. "Feedback" is not listed in the *Shorter Oxford Dictionary* or in Eric Partridge's *Origins,* which are my most familiar sources of word meanings and origins. However, I found it in the *American Heritage Dictionary* along with a quote from Norbert Weiner, the developer of cybernetics who may have invented the word. While I was looking up the word my children became curious. Usually the books I have in my study provide me with the information I need and here was a word in their dictionary that my larger one didn't have. They wanted to know what feedback was and I tried to explain that it had to do with ways of correcting things that you did when they went wrong. My words made no sense, I had to show them something that would embody the idea. Over the past few years I've learned that young children can master the most complex concepts if we are smart enough to embody them in an action or a story and so I tried to explain feedback to my children who were then five, seven, and eight, by asking them to pretend that they were blind. Tonia closed her eyes and grabbed my hand. I told her to start walking across the room. As she was about to walk into a wall I gave her a tug and she turned. Then she continued and before she crashed into a chair I squeezed her hand again. Josh, who is five, got the point, and said that feedback must mean that you help someone when they make a mistake so that they can do better the next time.

Tonia picked up on it right away and added that blind people use dogs to give them feedback. At that point Erica wondered how deaf people got feedback about sounds. I explained to her that one of the reasons deaf people have such a hard time learning to speak is that they don't get feedback on the sounds they make.

We went on to talk about the fact that some machines have built-in feedback mechanisms and are self-regulating. Everyday examples are thermostats and flush toilets. If you set the thermostat on a gas furnace at 70° when the actual temperature is 65°, the gas flow increases. When the water flowing back into a flush toilet reaches the right level, the ball in the tank automatically closes the water valve and shuts off the water so there is no flooding.

### Feedback and Learning

This discussion on feedback with my children got me thinking about feedback and education. If feedback is essential to being able to keep yourself in balance and deal with mistakes without becoming panicked, it is a main component of learning. By exploring the idea with a group of fourth graders, I found that a discussion of feedback and self-regulation is very useful, especially for teachers who want to analyze the effectiveness of their work.

First my students and I examined a flush toilet. The children thought this seemed a silly thing to do at first. I asked them why the toilet didn't flood all the time. We watched the water empty and fill in the tank. Finally the students figured out how the mechanism worked. Next I asked them to close their eyes and I pushed the mechanism out of kilter. This caused the toilet to drip and make noise. Then I asked the students if they could figure out how to fix the toilet. They used their understanding of feedback to find out why the valve didn't turn off and in a few minutes had the toilet fixed. The idea was no longer silly to the student who said, "I bet my mom would pay me to do that."

After this little adventure, I asked the students to list activities that did and didn't involve feedback. One girl said she used feedback when she painted. She looked at her work while she was painting and corrected things she didn't like. Another said he got feedback from his parents about everything he did, too much in fact, since they never let him do things for himself.

We also discussed the process of driving a car, which involves getting feedback all the time from the movement of the car in its response to braking, accelerating or turning the wheel. One student hit on an important idea in realizing that bad feedback might be the reason drunk drivers have so many accidents. We analyzed the effect of alcohol on the responses and the senses, and it became clear that as a result of drinking, the senses and nerves become dulled so that not enough information is received by the brain and what does come in is too slow to be useful.

### Feedback from Teachers
### to Students

One of the students commented that slow feedback was a problem in one of his classrooms. He said that everytime there was a fight the teacher broke it up but didn't discuss the problem until the next day. By that time, the students involved had forgotten about the issues or were ready to fight again.

At that point one of the girls jumped up and said she had an example of no feedback that bothered her. Grades. She felt that marks give no feedback because they don't help you correct mistakes or improve. She explained that just the day before, a paper came back from her teacher with a "B" and the comment "you can do much better" on it. She complained that this didn't help her know how to make the paper better and that she was frustrated. The other students agreed.

Our discussion made me think about my own work. How much feedback did I give to my students? How useful were my comments? How much feedback did they give me about the usefulness of my comments and grading system? I try not to grade work, but I have to admit there have been times when I have used phrases such as "very good" or "you could do better" as a way of getting through papers without taking them seriously. A few additional comments providing some real feedback to the students would have been much more helpful. For example, "Very good, but next time try to write this without using any words you don't have to. Try, if you have time, to see how many words you can cross out of this paper without changing the meaning." Or, "You could do better if you would think of who you were writing this for. Try writing it for your worst enemy and then for your best friend or your dog. Watch how the language changes."

I don't mean that it is never enough to say that some work is well done but rather that over the course of the year each student should get enough feedback on his or her work to know what has to be done to improve it. Thus, the goal of marking is to enable students to be self-regulating, to understand in concrete terms what is happening with their work and to teach themselves based on their teachers' comments.

### Feedback for Teachers

Another kind of feedback that is even rarer than that given to students is feedback on the quality of teachers' work. I have always felt that teaching in a public school can be a lonely experience no matter how good you are. You have to believe in yourself and your work, because you get little feedback from others except when you make mistakes.

Teachers have to find ways to get feedback. One way is to encourage your students to tell you about your work. You have to be careful to avoid asking your students to judge whether you are a good or bad teacher, but to be much more specific. For example, you can ask your students what subjects they find most interesting when you talk about them; ask them to tell you their favorite lessons; ask them to describe a time you taught something and they still didn't understand it and to suggest how you could make concepts clearer.

Another way to get feedback is to ask the students to play-act you teaching reading or math. Or ask them to take turns teaching a lesson the way you do or the way they would like to be taught. If you try these techniques you can get direct and indirect feedback that can make your work more interesting and challenging. In addition, the students will begin thinking about the processes of teaching and learning and give themselves feedback that will help themselves improve their own work.

### 2. Starting from Scratch

Starting from scratch consists of imagining how things first came to be. A good example is imagining with a group of children how measuring systems in general; and inches, feet, meters, and centimeters came to be. The imaginary reconstruction of a common human form can provide a model for the reconstruction of a current problem and the development of interesting solutions.

Several years ago I explored the reinvention of measuring systems with some children. I began by drawing this usual illusion on the board and asking whether the lines were the same size or not:

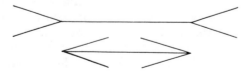

When one student guessed that both were the same size, I asked her to prove it. She laid a piece of paper along both lines, marking the beginning and the end of each, and showed me that they matched, proving by indirect comparison that they were the same size.

At that point, I explained there were other ways to measure things and asked one of the boys to trace his hand a number of times. Then by cutting out and taping the hands together, I made a "Ben's-hand" ruler and with it we measured a table.

All the students wanted to create their own measuring systems, and so Toni's hands and Charlie's feet and Celine's shoes all became units of measure. Soon the class saw the need to standardize measures, and Carol's hand was chosen by lot to be the standard for our class system.

I raised the problem of how we could measure an object smaller than Carol's hand. The students saw the need to break down the standard measure, so someone suggested that we use the length of Carol's thumb from the tip of the nail to the first joint as a smaller measure. It worked out beautifully since five of these units made up one "Carol's-hand." We had the beginning of a system of measurement with simple relationships between its parts.

Before long we needed a larger measurement to determine the length of the room and decided to call ten "Carol's-hands" a table, since that was just about the length of the tables in the room. Later the students developed a hundred-hand measure called a "room' and a two-room tape so that we could measure the playground and ball field and determine the length of paper airplane and glider flights.

Thus, our system, which started from scratch, evolved into the following form. The standard measure was Carol's hand traced on December 7, 1973. Its equivalents: 5 thumbs equal 1 hand; 10 hands equal 1 table; 10 tables, or 100 hands, equal 1 room.

Then I brought in some rulers containing both the metric and imperial systems. We talked about the two basic systems now used in the world to measure length and how trade and communication between people make it more practical to use just one system, metric, which seems easier to deal with.

My first-grade students had no trouble using and thinking in both systems. They also understood why more than one system had evolved because they had started from scratch and could imagine how other people developing systems of measurement could devise a variety of systems. They could see that measurement systems were the creative acts of real people, not abstract universal and unquestioned principles.

## Other Mathematical Systems

It is possible to build all kinds of math systems from scratch. For example, you can invent numerical symbols. Try adding and subtracting using only two or three symbols, without even mentioning the

notion of different base systems. I have found that ideas flow more freely
and understanding develops more easily when invention precedes exposure to already developed systems.

Inventing games, developing a notation to describe them, and then
trying to explore these games in an abstract sense, asking such questions as "Does the first or second grader have an advantage?" or "Is there
a way to play so that a win is guaranteed?" provides a good introduction
to mathematical systems and proof theory.

Starting from scratch can be equally effective in studying society or
culture or the individual psyche. The design of a city from scratch, the
creation of an imaginary history, the reconstruction of a nonexistent
culture, or the development of a psychological theory to explain certain
forms of behavior offers the insights and understanding that memorization or parroting other people's ideas cannot.

More specifically, in the case of the city, for example, one can prepare
the students to create a city by laying out the terrain; describing the
number and type of people who will settle it, the resources available, and
the wealth brought into the community; then letting the students go to
work trying to develop a self-sustaining congenial city.

It is also possible to reconstruct a culture using artifacts that are
incomplete clues from which the students try to recreate a whole
world—an altar, several utensils, a book of poems, a schoolbook, and a
map are good examples. It is even fun to give the same collection of
objects to several different groups of students and later have them
compare their reconstructions to see how material from our past, real or
imaginary, lends itself to many imaginative reconstructions.

All such problems are open-ended, and the students are limited only
by their imaginations, by their ability to share ideas with each other,
and by their teacher's patience and tolerance.

### Reading

Starting from scratch can also be utilized within the reading
curriculum. For example, create writing systems that transcribe the
way students speak, develop a gesture language, devise a notation to
describe pet communication, or construct a musical notation that includes noises made by cars and other machines as weil as a variety of
secret codes and languages.

Very young children can understand the relation between activities
(such as speaking) and abstract systems that are used to transcribe
them (such as our alphabet) if they are given a chance to develop some
such systems themselves and in that process to see the problems that

creation brings. Reading is too often mysterious to young children because they don't know what written symbols are getting at or how they were created.

## 3. Standing Things on Their Heads

This technique is especially useful for getting out of a rut and breaking a pattern of repeating mistakes. I often have found myself faced with students who just couldn't seem to grasp a crucial idea about reading or doing arithmetic. Frequently I responded by repeating the same thing over and over, becoming frustrated and hostile. I have learned to give up repetition and instead to try standing things on their heads.

### In the Curriculum

Often starting with an answer helps. Instead of asking someone to read a word, "frog" for example, tell the class that the word is "frog" and ask them to puzzle out why that particular word says frog.

Instead of asking what five and six equal, ask the students to think of all the different ways that two numbers can make up 11. Instead of requiring your students to try writing a perfect paper, it sometimes makes sense to ask them to write a paper in which they make as many mistakes as they can. After all, to know that one is making a mistake is not very different from knowing how to do something correctly.

I had one student who used to throw temper tantrums when asked to read. At first I tried to stop him by sitting him down firmly and lecturing him on how smart he was and on how he shouldn't be afraid of reading. Recently I instead asked him to cry louder and informed him that when he ran out of tears he'd be able to see the page better and read. It worked, and I do not believe that I was being cruel. Rather it is that I simply refused to reward him with my anger for behavior that is crippling to him. I have to stand things on their head.

### In Human Relations

In cases of group conflict, it often helps to stand things on their heads by acting out an event with all the roles reversed—boys and girls playing each other, Black and White children changing roles, a student playing teacher and the teacher playing student. I have also found this technique useful when preparing for confrontations. If my students want to confront another teacher or the principal or the school board, I have them role play the meeting, insisting that the students role play the different "adversaries" at least the first few times they act out the situation.

My intention is not to appease their anger (I believe there are times that one must oppose authority) but rather to show that people who dare to confront and change things need to understand as much as they can how the other people involved feel and to anticipate their responses to pressure.

## 4. Recombining the Elements

This is one of the fundamental strategies used by creative artists and scientists. Significant artistic and scientific works are never wholly new. Rather these works consist of bold and unexpected recombinations of what has gone before—forged into new ways of perceiving the world.

### Arts and Sciences

In the elementary school there are many materials that provide some exposure to this strategy: tangrams, puzzles, visual illusions, discovery units in science or math. Often, however, material not intended to foster creative vision can be used in different ways. There are many sequence stories that require students to put a series of pictures in the right order and then answer questions about the story. If imagination is allowed to overcome the literal mind, it is possible to put the pictures in a random order and make up a story to fit any sequence.

The same is true for words. There is, for example, an exercise with first graders that seems to enable them to think more freely and creatively. Each student in turn says a word (any word each wants), which I write on the chalkboard. An abbreviated list might read: red, mommy, first, sleep, stop, car, day, lunch, Hot Wheels.

After we complete the list, we consider some combinations and give the words some sense no matter how disconnected they initially seem. Usually we go down the list and start with two words at a time. Thus, we would read and talk about red-mommy, first-sleep, stop-car, day-lunch. Then we expand to three words at a time: red-mommy-first, sleep-stop-car, day-lunch-hot, Wheels.

The students don't find it difficult to fuse the images the words represent, and after a few weeks of doing this, I suggest that this fusion of images can be part of their writing just as it is part of much contemporary (and classical) poetry.

### Social Sciences

In dealing with economics and politics, recombining the elements is not only a good mind exercise but also a practical necessity if we are to solve and to help our children solve with us the problems facing the society.

One way to do this is to present students with an analysis of an actual situation—a city or community or nation in a state of crisis. Then the students can recombine the elements present in the situation to create a human solution to the problem of people living and growing together.

For example, a ghettoized city in the United States can be studied in terms of total resources available to the community—rich, poor, and in the middle. Or, a developing nation struggling to build up its own economy and independence can be studied.

Of course, the honesty and effectiveness of this kind of study will depend on the teacher's willingness to entertain bold, even revolutionary, redistributions of power and wealth. Students may also consider ideas that are more rigid than your own. Their mental development and freedom to grow, to uncover and explore their own values and to express their thoughts in an atmosphere of trust, without fear of censorship, will free them to imagine and create.

## 5. The Toystore of the Imagination

Recently I was a parent representative on a teacher selection committee for my children's school. During the course of our interviews with prospective teachers, there were times when we all reached for a significant question that would help us get a quick sense of what the interviewees were like as people. We wanted to know something about their interests beyond the classroom. One committee member asked a question that opened up a whole range of thinking exercises for me. The question was: If you had access to an enormous library containing every book that was ever written, what one book would you choose to read?

This challenge reminded me of a question I have asked myself from time to time. If I had to travel to a place where I knew there were no books and where none could be ordered, which five books would I take with me? Arriving at an answer has always helped me get a sense of the current state of my own thinking and needs. So I decided to ask a number of young people what books they would choose.

### A Place for Imaginations

The first children I asked happened to be second and third graders, and their answers set me off in a different direction than I had originally intended. They said that they would rather take toys and games than books on their trip. This response led me to conceive of "the toy store of the imagination." It's important, at any age, to have a time and vehicle to use our imagination without worrying about whether the ideas are right, wrong or even possible. The toy store of the imagination is such a vehicle. It is a place where all the games and toys you ever have seen or imagined exist. In it one might find games where the players become mini-people who take the place of game pieces, or games in which players can be transported through space and time. In the toy store of the imagination toys take any form imaginable. Because they are controlled by your mind, they can walk, talk, and fly. They can even make and invent new toys themselves.

### More Than Just Toys

When I asked some older students what they would like to get from a toy store of the imagination, they had ideas that went beyond playthings. One boy cited a "self-writing pencil." He explained that his pencil would write automatically whatever was in his mind that he wanted it to. He could think out a story, a math example or a sentence for a spelling word; then, when he was ready, the pencil would write down his thoughts.

One of the girls said she would like to have two-inch-tall friends she could carry around in her pocket. Other children added the following personal aid ideas:

> A machine that would make food that wouldn't make you fat
>     or give you pimples
> A homework-explaining machine
> An "unrunoutable" ballpoint pen
> Self-fetching firewood

One child who had braces added that she would like an automatic, nonhurting, one-minute tooth straightener.

### Ideas and More Ideas

By examining the lists I collected from first through sixth graders I got a number of ideas about how the toys-of-the-imagination curriculum could be elaborated on or expanded. Why not set up an inventors' workshop in the classroom? For example, one boy said he would like to have a car that could turn itself into an airplane or a boat. There's no reason he couldn't sketch or even construct a wooden or cardboard model of such a vehicle.

Another student said she would like to play "Monopoly" with a real city. Instead of using tiny hotels, motels and other pieces, she imagined life-size players and buildings. We couldn't build a city for her "Monopoly" game, but through our inventors' workshop we *could* create some simple game boards in the schoolyard and use students themselves as the game pieces.

A simple version of such a game would be "Real-Life Tic-Tac-Toe." You and your students could draw a great big tic-tac-toe board on the ground. Then the children could form two groups, one with five players wearing "X" labels; the other with four wearing "Os." Next, the players would line up on either side of the board and the first "X" (or "O") would move onto the board. Then the first "O" (or "X") would move on, and so on until one side won or tied the game. One of the other students could be the judge and call tic-tac-toe for a winner. On a grander scale, you could play life-size chess and checkers, inventing interesting ways to act out captures and moves.

An inventors' workshop needn't produce models but could instead depend upon drawing and writing descriptions of how to go about creating toys of the imagination. Edward De Bono, an inventor himself, posed some interesting problems to children that required them to use their inventive intelligence. He reported on the inventions the children created in response in his marvelous book *Children Solve Problems* (Harper & Row). Some of the creative exercises he asked children to do included:

> Design a fun machine.
> If you were a zoo keeper, how would you find out the weight of
>     an elephant?
> Design a special bed for people who have difficulty going to
>     sleep.
> Draw a picture showing how you could make your body better.

## Unreal Ideas
## Solve Real Problems

Using De Bono's technique you could ask students to draw pictures of the toys they have chosen from the toy store of the imagination and even to design the store itself. I have been working with some of my students on an elaborate design that includes a number of different departments. One will be called "Toys and Other Gadgets that Make Life at School Easier." Next to that section will be one called "Chore-Doing Toys and Other Devices that Make Life at Home Easier." There will also be a section on travel that contains, among other things, invisibility pills; miniaturization powder; and tiny rockets, cars, and boats in which Tom Thumb-size people can travel.

Exploring the realm of the imaginable through the device of a toy store is creative and fun, but it can also lead to some serious discussions. Many times in inventing toys and gadgets students describe things they actually need to solve their own real problems. For example, the homework-explaining machine that one of my students wanted led to an interesting discussion about how it is sometimes hard to understand or remember your assignment once you get home.

In the course of the conversation, one student suggested that teachers tape explanations of homework assignments and put them on a telephone answering system. You could call it any time you needed to be reminded of what you have to do. Everyone agreed that this was a good idea. One student added that it would also solve the problem of finding out what the homework was when you were absent.

The discussion did not lead to taped homework messages, but it did lead some students to ask their teachers if they could call them at home about homework. Most teachers didn't object if calls were made at reasonable times. A real problem was solved by starting with an imaginary solution.

The toy store of the imagination is only one device for helping students free themselves of inhibitions and letting their minds and imaginations go. You can invent others. For example:

• You are going on a magical journey to live on a hot, remote island for one year. You can only take one suitcase with you. You can have anything you can fit in that suitcase, including some things that may not have been invented yet. What would you pack in the case? Remember, they have to be things, not wishes.

• You have just inherited an inventors' workshop from your aunt and uncle who designed on request any gimmick or gadget that anyone desired. It is almost Christmas and you want to give special presents. Make a list describing in words and/or pictures the inventions that you would give to your friends and members of your family. Make sure your creations have never been seen, much less owned. Try to make the presents fit the people.

You are a magical biologist. You have the power to create in your laboratory any life forms you can imagine. What creatures would you put in the world? How would they live and survive? What creatures would you not dare to create?

### 6. The Positive
### Use of Negative Thinking
### or Ten Ways Not to . . .

One particularly rainy day I faced a restless resistant class. There didn't seem to be any way to get them to write or talk. I suggested all kinds of interesting themes for writing, asked them if they had any favorite jokes or stories. Nothing worked. Finally, in desperation, I asked them to each make a list of ten reasons why they couldn't write. They set to work immediately, a few laughing as they realized that they were doing just what they had said they couldn't do.

#### How Not to Write

The lists the students came up with indicated how aware they were of the dynamics of learning—and avoiding learning. Here are ten of their "Ten Ways Not to Write":

1. Talk about how you can't write.
2. Start with a subject or story idea that's too hard and then worry about it.
3. Break your pencil and ask for another.
4. Pretend you're writing.
5. Put down any words and then erase them.
6. Look serious.
7. Go to the toilet.
8. Sweat and have clammy hands.
9. Try to get everything right the first time.
10. Be bad.

We talked about the lists. It seemed as if all the students had thought about the psychological context of learning, but they had never talked about it before. Some of the students said that they were afraid to write;

others said that they'd rather write with no one looking at them. As the discussion developed, it turned out that the students did want to write but that they didn't know how to go about it without anxiety.


### How to Write

Next, I took the list-making a step further and asked each of the children to make a list of "Ten Ways to Write." In thinking through these lists the students began to identify things that would make learning most comfortable for them. Here are ten from these lists of ten:

1. Not having to worry about doing something right or wrong.
2. Not having to show the paper to anyone until I'm ready.
3. Having someone look at my paper to help me without marking it.
4. Knowing I can start a couple of times instead of only once.
5. Having music on so I can relax.
6. Having it quiet so I can think.
7. Having the chance to do a lot of writing and then pick the best to show.
8. Having more than one topic I can choose to write about.
9. Having the opportunity to take notes in class and write the paper at home.
10. Having the chance to walk around and talk about some of the things I want to write before writing.

I found that these and the other responses gave me and the teacher I was working with a sense of the framework we had to build to help our students learn to write with ease.


### How Not to Play Basketball

I had an occasion to use a variation of the "Ten Ways Not to . . ." method this summer. Some girls wanted to learn to play basketball so they could try out for the school team in the fall, and I agreed to help them out. The first day on the court they kept complaining about how they simply couldn't play basketball. They kept telling each other how they wanted to play but knew they couldn't. At this point, I threw them the ball and suggested that they show me ten ways in which they couldn't play basketball. One girl ran up to the basket and threw the ball behind her instead of toward the basket. Another rolled the ball slowly across the court instead of passing it. It was clear that the girls had been watching basketball. Apparently they had thought so much about how they would play that they were too nervous to actually begin and learn by making mistakes. When I started with the negative and let them articulate their fears, the girls were able to come in contact with the ball, laugh about their mistakes and start to learn to play basketball.

There are many ways negative lists can help anyone focus on problems and arrive at solutions. For example, a number of teachers I work with have been hit with budget cuts, the prospect of loss of tenure and the failure of school bond issues. In this climate they have felt demoralized (especially here in California where the passage of Proposition 13 has forced statewide cuts and layoffs). In such a context we have found it all the more important to be positive about our work and to try to build community confidence and support.

To help ourselves analyze our feelings and overcome depression a number of other teachers and I have begun lists of "Ten Reasons Why I Can't Teach Well This Year." Ten of the reasons we have come up with so far are:

1. The administrators won't let me.
2. There isn't enough money to buy the new program I want.
3. The students aren't motivated.
4. The climate isn't ripe for change.
5. I tried that before and it didn't work.
6. All that parents care about are the basic skills.
7. Because there are too many students in my class I can't be creative.
8. I don't have enough time to plan.
9. The materials I need aren't on the approved list.
10. Nobody will appreciate what I do anyway.

For each of these ten reasons we can't teach well we have tried to come up with ten ways we can teach well—overall, "100 Ways to Do the Best We Can for Children Whatever the Surrounding Conditions." Here are our ten answers to number six, "All that parents care about are the basic skills":

1. Think about what I really believe the basic skills are and try to teach them in my own way.
2. Agree with parents about the importance of basic skills, but tell them that there are many ways to teach these

skills and that as an experienced professional I have to use the techniques that work best for me.

3. Share my concerns with a friend who is also a teacher.
4. Tell my principal the great things my students are doing and keep him or her informed about how well they are learning the basics.
5. Teach reading through film, radio drama, and improvisation.
6. Teach writing through comic books and novels and writing as if I were making a speech to Congress or announcing a baseball game.
7. Teach math by using loan applications, car ads, apartment or house leases, batting averages, and the *Guiness Book of World Records*.
8. Bring in the widest possible range of reading materials.
9. Have my students create and publish their own books and sell them to raise money for class projects.
10. Read, write, and do some math myself.

Here's another list of ten positive responses to number 7, "Because there are too may students in my class I can't be creative." It was sent to me by Katherine T. Cane who read the "Ten Ways Not to . . ." column:

1. Refocus goals with the realization that the creativity in the classroom that is most vital to encourage is *student* creativity.
2. Remember that an overwhelmingly creative teacher may well stifle the children in their quest to discover what their own creativity can produce.
3. Consider that each additional child in the classroom adds to the total spectrum of creativity in the group.
4. Come to understand that creativity is "common" . . . a natural part of each learning experience. It need not be viewed as a "frill".
5. Present open-ended activities which require input by the students rather than a teacher-created finale.
6. Demand a time to create during routine class time—a time set apart as creative learning time for the students, as well as creative teaching time.
7. Give more responsibility to the students in directing the course various topics of study may take. They will provide more creative thought than a single teacher can possibly contrive. This often simply takes *listening*!
8. Try to avoid presenting material in a way which leads the students to presume that you are assigning set expectation for the way the material is to be approached. Often by simply giving

written material without pictures or pictures without dialogue, the material presented abounds with possibilities.

9. Make sure that you are not expecting a specific end (and no alternative) to *each* task assigned and you will be adding a creative allowance to the limits of the assignments.

10. Make available a tremendous supply of matrials which promote creativity simply through their availability to the students. Often the most creative thing you can do as a teacher is to provide opportunities to explore learning that is not required!

## 7. The Uses Of Ignorance

Several months ago, while browsing in our local bookshop, I came across a book with an intriguing title—*The Encyclopedia of Ignorance: Everything You Always Wanted to Know About the Unknown,* edited by Ronald Duncan and Miranda Weston-Smith (Pocket Books). On first glance I assumed it was about the occult or was a parody of other "Everything you wanted to know about . . ." books. The index, however, made it clear that this was an extremely serious attempt to explain current unsolved problems in the sciences and mathematics. Here's a sampling of chapter headings: "Leaf Structure and Function" "The Riddles of Gravitation" "Some Unsolved Problems in Higher Mathematics" and "Why We Do Not Understand Pain".

I bought the book and am still working my way through it as some of the articles are quite technical. Nevertheless, the idea of an encyclopedia of ignorance raises many interesting questions having to do with the present limits of knowledge. I decided to explore some of them with a group of fourth-, fifth- and sixth-graders. As teachers we spend almost all of our school time talking with young people about what adults already know. The subject of ignorance rarely comes up; yet it is out of intelligent definitions of the unknown that many significant discoveries arise.

### Just Plain Stupid

I began by talking with my students about the distinction between ignorance and stupidity. We agreed that stupidity is when you know the consequences of an act or the facts about a situation, but use them without malicious intent in a way that produces negative results. One student gave the example of throwing a baseball through the window of your house to show off to friends. You know the ball will break the window. You know your parents will be angry. You probably also know you will regret what you did later, but you do the stupid thing anyway.

Our discussion went on to clarify the difference between stupidity and ignorance. One girl asked whether polluting the environment wasn't stupid. She said it was just like throwing the ball through the window. We pollute the air, say, and after awhile find it hard to breathe. Then we regret having done whatever it was we did to pollute. Someone objected, saying that at first people didn't know what effects car exhaust and factory smoke would have on the air. They were ignorant of the consequences of the acts and, therefore, couldn't be called stupid. In other words, people became stupid about pollution; they didn't start out that way.

Next I asked each child to make a list of things he or she didn't know but might like to. Some of the responses from our individual lists were:

> I don't know why airplanes fly.
> I don't know how many people there are in the world.
> I don't know how to do long division.
> I don't know how my baby brother learned to talk.
> I don't know why I like some people and don't like others.
> I don't know why some art is called beautiful. (We had gone to
>   the museum together and had an argument over "modern
>   art," which most of the students had found ugly and silly.)
> I don't know how a book gets printed.

We sorted our lists into four categories, the first three being: things that we can learn from other people or books; skills that we can acquire; and things that we can discover by doing something, such as counting or measuring. What remained were the things that nobody knows for sure at this time.

It was a lot harder to categorize our lists than we had anticipated. For example, just look at the above samples. It took us some research to find out that we do have an adequate explanation for flight and that, though we couldn't know exactly how many people there are in the world at any given moment, good statistical guesses are possible After thinking about it, students realized that they could find out how to do long division by asking someone who knew or by consulting a textbook, and that they could learn how books are printed by checking in an encyclopedia or visiting a press. Three questions, however, which the students all expected would have easy answers were much more challenging. How does a baby learn to talk? Why do we like some people and not others? Why are some works of art called beautiful? These sent us on some interesting journeys.

### Baby Stuff

At first, most students said they were sure that a baby learned to talk by imitation and that they could prove this by looking in an encyclopedia or some library book. However, when I asked Joan, the student who posed the question, if her brother ever said a sentence he had not heard anyone else say, she said that he did it all the time. Thus we agreed that though imitation is involved it can't be all there is to learning a language. One of the older students looked up "language" in our edition of the *Encyclopedia Britannica* and came upon an unsatisfactory explanation: that at around the age of two children "somehow make sense" of language. The "somehow" was the key to ignorance.

I asked one student to look in the library for books on linguistics and another to call a psychology department of a local college and ask a professor if anyone knew how language was learned. The students thought my suggestion that they call a college was crazy. They had never thought of college professors as learning resources. But I pushed the idea. Finally, three students agreed to talk to someone at the college if I would dial the number for them and explain their purpose in "bothering" a professor.

The professor we reached was delighted with our request and sent a graduate student to visit us. She gave us a fascinating short talk on the current state of knowledge about how people acquire language. She said that no one really knows how people learn to speak, or read for that matter, but that bits and pieces about the process are known. She also said that there are a number of different theories about learning to speak. She added that what made the field of linguistics exciting for her was that there is still so much to be known. The more ignorance there is in a field of learning, the more room there is for creativity and exploration.

One student asked our visitor whether our other unanswered questions were also, as he put it, "somewhere in the land of ignorance." She said she wasn't sure, but that there were people in the fields of psychology and art who would be able to address those questions. She also said that it was nice to talk about the limits of her field since it gave her a chance to think and guess. She even shared some of her feelings about learning language with us.

As we continued, we found out that there are as many theories about how people choose friends and about the nature of beauty in art as there are about learning language. The students realized that uncertainty and ignorance exist in these fields, as well.

### The Next Step

Now we are trying to decide how to follow up on our initial explorations of ignorance. Among a number of ways, we could pursue the open-ended questions we raised, investigating linguistics, psychology, and aesthetics (to the degree possible given the students' current state of sophistication). Such a course could lead us to find out what parts of our questions have been answered, to consider current theories and to speculate on answers. We wouldn't have to come up with the correct answer and we wouldn't expect to. The speculation itself would provide significant learning.

I've discussed this possible course of study with a number of teachers and other colleagues and most of them are skeptical. They think that the subject matter would be too complex for fourth, fifth, and sixth graders. I'm not so sure, and their skepticism tempts me to go ahead and try. I don't know how far middle-grade students can go with the limits of current knowledge, but I am sure that I would learn at least as much as they in the attempt.

### The Meaning of Life

Another way we might continue our explorations is to identify ignorance in other areas of learning. For example, what are current unknowns in biology? There are some obvious ones, such as how was life created in the first place?

Other questions have to do with evolution. How do life forms diversify? Is evolution only a struggle for survival or does altruism play a part in the creation of the species? And what about the world? How did it begin and how might it end? On a more immediate level, what are the effects of resource depletion on the earth? What do we know about predicting the future? What does choice mean in people's lives? How much energy can the sun provide? The sea? The wind? Is it possible for people to live without conflict in groups?

Many, perhaps most, of these and other basic questions are still unanswered, and my students and I could spend time articulating them, finding out how much is currently known and speculating on ways of carrying the answers further. My experience with young students has convinced me that they are capable of dealing with such important questions. I believe that the thought involved in considering the unknown can lead children as young as nine or ten to eventually develop a critical awareness that they can use in other school subjects and in dealing with all the unknowns of everyday life.

# C
# *Resistance to Learning*

This section deals with overcoming the failure syndrome in students who feel they simply cannot learn what is expected of them.

*F*or some children it is easier to fail than to try to succeed. Recently I encountered two very different examples of children who seemed determined to fail. Benjamin was very shy and almost invisible in class. He always hovered on the margin of failure. He avoided paticipating in discussion, wandered off by himself on the playground and usually turned in his work late and half complete. He was no trouble to anyone but himself and constantly had adults feeling sorry for him. Victor, on the other hand, was loud and provocative. He didn't flirt with failure; he embraced it. He couldn't do anything well in class except threaten students who tried to make fun of him.

I started to work with both of these boys in a group setting and noticed that, as superficially different as they were, their behavior was similar in a number of ways. For example, when given a choice of projects they always chose the most difficult and called the simple ones "baby stuff." However, halfway through the projects they both found ways of quitting: Benjamin by disappearing quietly or simply refusing to work and Victor by provoking a fight or destroying what he had already done. When confronted with their failures they never made excuses; they simply told me that they were stupid and that that was all there was to it. They both accepted failure as a way of life.

It was hard working with Benjamin and Victor in a group context. They commanded more time than all the other students combined because both continually needed to have their negative sense of themselves confirmed. Whenever I was occupied with other students, Benjamin began to mope with a vengeance and moved as close to me as possible. At the same time, Victor's tone got louder and louder. Basically they were both doing the same thing: trying to get rewards for failing. I gradually began to realize that I was playing into their hands by giving Benjamin so much sympathy and by constantly reacting to Victor's outbursts and interruptions. As this dawned on me, it became clear that for the sake of those two, and the rest of the students as well, I had to find a way of reaching those boys that would integrate them into the class and confront them with situations in which they could not fail.

As I thought about the problem, several realizations helped me plan a strategy to undo the failure syndrome of the two boys. First I realized that offering Benjamin sympathy and chasing Victor would never help. Second, I realized that it was at certain crucial moments—usually right after they had done preliminary work and had to move to a slightly more complex phase of the projects—that they started attacking, destroying, or abandoning their work. I decided that that moment was the time to intervene and force them to succeed.

### Two Strategies

Through work with these two boys and others like them, I've learned that there are ways to force success upon students who are accustomed to failure. Two very simple—but within a general context disapproved—strategies usually work. One, give the students the answers; two, do the work for them. That does not mean to give the students all the answers or do all their work for them. What it means is that in situations where students are accustomed to quitting, you have to get them over the hump. For example, students with writer's block sometimes need you to write a first sentence for them, or to write a sentence in the middle of the story that will get them out of a "dead end."

Sometimes in math, students need you to sit down and slowly work out a problem for them while they watch. I believe that demonstrating a problem and participating in a student's work is part of teaching. It's important to show the students you are with them, will help them along as they learn and not merely give instruction and then test for the results. This technique of teaching is used by a number of Native American cultures: One teaches by doing something in front of a child very slowly and provides him or her with the opportunity of copying. One trusts the child to learn by watching.

### How to Help

In working with Benjamin and Victor it became clear to me that I would have to sit with them at times. I would do their work for them, demonstrating what had to be done and then letting them copy me while I made sure they got the right answers. I hoped they would learn by watching and gain courage if I showed them that I, too, made mistakes in struggling to get things right. Also, I hoped that if I chose the right moments, the boys would learn to wait for the special time I gave them and let me give time to the other children in the class as well.

A third thing I had to do was somehow rout the word "stupid" out of their vocabulary. An opportunity to work on this came up soon. One student in the class (not Victor or Benjamin) called another "retarded," and a whole group of children started laughing. At that point I called a class meeting and wrote the word "retarded" on the chalkboard in capital letters. I asked the class what the word meant, and some of the answers were "stupid," "dumb," "idiotic," "crazy," "wierd," "silly." I then asked the students if all those words meant the same thing.

We talked about the precise meanings of "moron," "retardation," "dumbness," and "stupidity." Then I made up a story about how people find ways of controlling others by making them believe they are inferior.

Finally, making sure not to look at either Victor or Benjamin, I said that the worst part of being called stupid is that some people finally believe it and start calling *themselves* stupid. I told the class that doing that was a way of allowing other people to control you, a form of weakness not a sign of strength. Then I challenged the class to go a week without using any such words to insult each other.

From that time on, I could see a change in Victor and Benjamin. When they called themselves "stupid," which they did rarely, they didn't seem to be insulting themselves. They seemed to recognize that they were doing it to avoid work. I think that now they realized that by allowing others to believe they were stupid, they were allowing themselves to be controlled.

I strongly believe that there are times when we as teachers have the responsibility to forcefully undo damage done to our students by the words or actions of other adults or children. We have to let our students know that they are *not* stupid and that *we*, their teachers, are there to strengthen and support them as they learn rather than to categorize them and tear them down.

### A Breakthrough

Of course eliminating the word "stupid" did not eliminate the problem, and I had to implement the other part of my plan. I watched the boys carefully as they began projects. I gave them no more time than I did the other students, but fortunately my class is set up so that most students can work independently after awhile, and I had time to intervene when I saw that either Benjamin or Victor was about to give up.

The first breakthrough came with Victor. He was trying some math problems. As usual, he had picked something that was too difficult for him—automatically programming himself for failure. He had started an algebra workbook I had made available for students who already had a strong command of arithmetic. I watched Victor out of the corner of my eye as I answered other students' questions. He did the first page easily, but the material on the next page was too complex for him.

As soon as I began to see that Victor was getting frustrated and angry, I went over to him and sat down. I did the second page of algebra for him, writing my calculations out on another sheet of paper. I gave him that paper and told him to use what I had done, copying it if necessary, as a guide. There was no legitimate way he could fail. All he had to do was reproduce my work.

Victor seemed a bit puzzled by what I was doing but accepted the answers and copied them. Then before he could go onto the next page, which I knew would be frustrating for him, I told him he had done enough good work for that day. Then I took the book to keep for him, protecting his work from his own destructive tendencies. The next day I asked him to begin by redoing the last page he had done on the day before and said I would help him with new work.

Little by little, Victor seems to be coming out of his self-hatred and at the same time calming down. Recently instead of tearing up the story he was writing, he asked for help with it. He is also fighting less and taking up less of the class's time with his demands.


### Working Together

Things have begun to change for Benjamin, too. The change began when the whole class was engaged in designing a city "for kids, of kids, and by kids." I had brought in a number of books on futuristic architecture to stimulate new ideas and expose students to contemporary building design. After the class planned all aspects of their city together, they chose specific projects to work on.

Benjamin chose the most difficult project of all: a circular apartment building built around a central core that housed a park, stores, and restaurants. I suggested that he try something simpler, but he insisted and began to lay out the apartment building.

He began well, but after awhile I noticed that he had slowed down and that his eyes had begun to wander.He had been trying to build a circular building and then something else in the middle of it before it was even finished. One activity was negating the other. At that point I asked him what the trouble was. He replied typically: "It won't work; I can't do it; I'm stupid; it's no use." I tried to direct his attention away from himself and let him focus on the project. I insisted that he be specific. "What won't work? What have you tried to do to make it work? How do you think *we* could go about doing it?"

We decided that he would build the apartment separately from the park and stores and put them together later. In addition to talking about his plans, I helped him lay the foundations for his apartment house. Then, it seemed necessary to do the same thing I'd done with Victor's work. I took it and kept it in a special place to return to him the next day. Until he could assume full responsibility for his work, I had to show him that I would support him by assuming responsibility for its safety myself.

### Don't Let Students Fail

I think it's important to rethink the role of teacher. To help children who have the greatest needs, we sometimes have to do the most unexpected things: give the answers, do work for and with them, and explicitly explain to them how they are hurting themselves. Sometimes, as with Benjamin and Victor, we have to *make sure* our students succeed instead of merely testing to see if they have succeeded.

# D
# Being Indirect

On ways to use stories, jokes, and other face-saving devices to help insecure students develop strength and intelligence.

*H*ere is a series of techniques to encourage learning without having to resort to harsh discipline or verbal humiliation:

## 1. The Grouch Factor

Sometimes students cannot handle direct criticism, especially if their friends are present. When I first started teaching, my impulse was to confront students directly as soon as they acted in ways that made life difficult for the rest of us. If someone was shouting out in the middle of a quiet reading time, or harassing another student who was trying to work I'd tell him immediately and unambiguously to stop. Often I found myself in the middle of a "you will"–"I won't" no-win situation that could only be solved by removing the student or by physical confrontation. Since neither of these techniques helped the students or me as a teacher I began to evolve indirect strategies for dealing with classroom disruptions.

One particular strategy developed while I was teaching first grade in Berkeley. One of the students in the class last year called me "Herbie, the Grouch" every time I got angry at him. This particular boy, David, sometimes came in sullen and angry, would push other children out of his way, hit them in the back or knock over their games and scribble on their work. But on other days, he would be the gentlest, most charming and considerate person. It was impossible to tell from one day to the next what his mood would be.

I took to watching him walk into the room in the morning. In our class the students come in a few at a time, and for the first hour they can choose from many different activities. During that hour the students have individualized reading; thus we have a chance to spend a few minutes a day with every child.

David was usually the first student I called to read, or at least the one I looked at first. I watched the way he walked into the room, noted the set of his brow, how he held his hands and fists, how his eyes scanned the room. At the first sign of aggression I pounced:

"David, today you'll take care of yourself. . . ."
"David you read first today. . . ."
"David keep your hands to yourself. . . ."
"David do something . . . sit down . . . enjoy yourself. . . ."
"David don't. . . ."

"Grouch, grouch, grouch." That's what he called me, and the other students picked up on it, too. I didn't like being called a grouch and tried to joke off the name. However, I couldn't let him continue to harass the other students and destroy their work. I had to accept a minimally "grouchy" role in order to allow the other students the peace and calm they needed to make choices and function in our open environment.

It became easy after awhile to set limits on David's behavior by "sitting on top of him at the beginning of the day." But there were problems with my behavior. Sometimes I came to school tired and impatient and found myself grouching at David and some of the other students in the hope that it would make my day easier.

The difference between grouching to set and maintain sensible limits in the class—to ensure that bullying and destruction of work didn't develop—and grouching just to make my day easier wasn't always clear. I could sense something was wrong on those days because some of the students would imitate me and they, too, would go around complaining at the slightest thing. Those days we were a tired and very touchy group.

Teachers are sometimes tired, obsessed, and troubled by things that have nothing to do with events in the classroom. It is impossible to conceal these feelings, especially in an informal learning environment in which the adults and young people have the time to talk to each other. Ways have to be found to bring these feelings out in the open rather than try to force silence and obedience on the class so the teacher can relax.

The students would occasionally tell me to turn the grouch off, pointing out that they hadn't done anything wrong. They showed me that on some days I let them play around or make noise and that on other days I didn't.

David suggested the grouch factor was located somewhere in the back of my brain. Picking up on his suggestion, I drew a head and a brain on the chalkboard. At the back of the brain, I labeled a section the grouch's house. We began to discuss what brought out the grouch in me and in others as well. The idea of a "grouch" allowed many of the students to acknowledge that they, too, had grouch days.

We decided that there were inside and outside reasons that set the grouch off. I admitted that at times I grouched because I came to school in a bad mood and at other times because I had to set limits on some of the students' behavior. David acknowledged that he woke up some mornings with his grouch out, and on those mornings it seemed as if his grouch activated mine.

The discussion was quite sophisticated, certainly more so than I had suspected five- and six-year-olds capable of. We were able to use the grouch idea as an image to enable us to think about and analyze behavior patterns. The notion of a grouch factor even changed some people's behavior in the classroom.

One day we speculated on what keeps the grouch happy—jokes, snacks, praise, isolation. We talked about ways we had of bringing angry feelings under control. I suggested that the students remind me when my grouch was showing and told them I would do the same.

It was no longer necessary for me to look at David for signs of aggression or to put a moral interpretation on his behavior. (Despite myself he was emerging in my mind as a "bad" student even though he was one of the most intelligent and competent students in the class.) It was his grouch factor, and I could appeal to it when he came in angry.

Moreover, since it was *his* grouch he began to assume responsibility for his behavior and learned ways to leave other students alone or scribble on his own work or go outside and break a stick instead of a game or a sculpture. The students could also remind me of my feelings, and I could deal with them without feeling insulted or injured by the students' criticism.

Indirect ways of discussing feelings help decharge a situation. I have found that young children use superheroes, animals, imaginary friends, and astrological symbols as tokens that enable them to deal in complex ways with pain and conflict, as well as to assume responsibility for their own behavior. Whenever some collective problem arises in our class, I have found that the best way to deal with it is to start with a story, fable, or adventure that embodies the problem. Then we can deal with the problem in the class through the story, causing no one to lose face and everyone to be able to talk about responsibility.

### 2. Earth, Air, Fire, and Water

Classical symbols of personality make useful categories for indirect discussions of serious personal and group problems. To the ancient Greeks, all of nature was made up of four elements—earth, air, fire, and water. These elements were the subject of scientific investigation; they were represented in paintings and described and invoked in poetry and music. Even today, all of us have associations with these elements and preferences for one or other of them. These associations and preferences can be used as a handle for opening up classroom discussion.

One way to begin is by telling students about the elements and the way in which some people felt they constituted the world. Then ask the students to freely associate with each of the elements and put their associations on the board. Something like this usually results:

> *Earth:* Warm, dirty, seed, brown, rich, green.
> *Air:* Thin, pure, fly, high, colorless, open, head.
> *Fire:* Heat, burn, hurt, passion, feel, love, die.
> *Water:* Swim, cool, drown, float, calm, storm.

After that talk about the associations, and about the differences that exist among the elements, ask students to put down in order the elements they feel closest to. Do the same thing yourself, and then look at the class responses and see what preferences are. Have students look at each other's responses. There are no right and wrong answers, it is all a matter of personal preferences. It was interesting that in the class most of the boys preferred air and fire, and most of the girls preferred earth and water. For the Greeks air and fire were masculine elements, and earth and water, feminine.

After we examined everyone's preferences I asked the class to assume that they were each composed of some mixture of earth, air, fire, and water and to make up charts of their own percentages. The students really got into thinking about themselves and became curious about each other's choices. Later a student suggested that someone in the class leave the room and make up a chart about himself in the hall while everyone else made up their own charts on him. Then we could compare what the person thought of himself with how others perceived him, as in the chart below.

| Jenny–Three Perceptions | | |
|---|---|---|
| | Jenny sees herself | Teacher sees Jenny | Jon sees Jenny |
| Earth | 10% | 25% | 10% |
| Air | 10% | 25% | 10% |
| Fire | 50% | 25% | 30% |
| Water | 30% | 25% | 50% |

I made no attempt to interpret what the students said about each other and themselves. They understood certain things and accepted the exercises as nonjudgmental. There were no right nor wrong responses, no marks involved. It was fun, they looked at each other and also at me as a person responding in the same way they responded. The students were able to get away from being passive in the classroom and from competing with each other. It was also possible for students who were causing discipline problems to talk about themselves, about, for example, their fiery natures and the need for more water in their nature to quench their tempers.

The results of indirect conversations like these are usually not immediate but they provide openings for sensible dialogue with students who have problems with self-control. They also give students images of themselves which can be useful in developing new, and more socially integrated ways of behaving.

### 3. Social Maps

Social maps (what are generally called sociograms), are also good tools for self-analysis and nonthreatening discussions of maintaining discipline within a group.

A few years ago September and October were very difficult months in my fifth-grade classroom. These particular students and I never seemed to cohere as a group. There were cliques that fought among themselves, petty jealousies and constant arguments. At times I wondered if I could be the source of the trouble. However, I was full of energy, well-prepared and liked the students individually. I could only ascribe the difficulties to the group's chemistry.

Each time I tried to talk to the class as a whole about our problems, everyone denied there was anything basically wrong and yet blamed the bad atmosphere on other students. No one seemed to have a sense of the group as a whole or show any willingness to talk about the role they played within it.

One day, in desperation, I gave each student a large piece of drawing paper and wrote everyone's name, including my own, on the chalkboard. My list was in alphabetical order to avoid the complaints I had come to expect from this group. Then I asked the children to draw a "name map" of the class showing who hung out with who and who liked and didn't like each other. I also asked the students to include me on the map in any way they felt I belonged. I asked them to begin by writing their own names on any part of the paper that seemed right to them and then to add names of people that they felt were close to them. I stressed that it was important to imagine that the blank piece of paper, or map, represented social relationships, not the physical space we shared in the room.

To my surprise the whole class was quiet for the first time during the year. The idea of making a social map of our life together was intriguing to everyone. I, too, took a blank piece of paper and tried to figure out where I belonged in that social space—certainly not in the center of the page nor totally in a corner. I put my name somewhere to the left of center. As I began to fill in the names of students, I realized that certain groups seemed to fit more naturally on my side of the paper and others belonged farther away on the other side. Furthermore, some of the students were not part of any of the groups I drew, and I isolated these in the corners of the page. There were two children I couldn't place at all. In all my anxiety about getting the class to cohere, I realized that I hadn't paid much attention to those two quiet children.

The map-making process was fascinating to the students, since it provided a visual form that allowed them to focus their thoughts on the social structure of the classroom. As the students finished, they began sharing their maps with each other. I suggested we copy some on the board and talk about them, and a few students volunteered.

### Rose's View

First I chose Rose, one of the most aggressive students in the class. Rose had put herself in the lower-left-hand corner of the paper surrounded by four other girls who were her closest friends. Opposite them in the lower-right-hand corner, she placed a group of five other girls. All the girls in Rose's group were Black. All those in the other group were White. (See the map below.)

In between the groups were five individuals—three boys and two girls—with my name above and to the left of them. On the upper-right-hand corner of the paper, not grouped very closely together, were the names of five of the White boys in the classroom. Rose explained to the class that these boys all seemed like loners. In the upper-left-hand corner was another group of five boys—four Black and one White. They were, according to Rose, the boys who hung out together.

I felt Rose's portrait was very accurate. Moreover it gave me a new view of the five students she had put in the middle. Thinking about it, I realized that they were the mediators in the room, the ones who related to and were respected by all the other students. I realized which students I could turn to when things were getting out of hand.

The isolation of a number of the White boys in the class was also revealing and quite troubling to me. As soon as Rose described why she had put them in the corner as "isolates," one of the boys complained that the reason he was so alone was that no one liked him. Another student responded that the reason the boy was alone was because he never shared anything and couldn't take a joke. Someone else added that he always acted as if someone stole something from him.

This was a lot for the child to take at one time, and he withdrew. However, I noticed that over the next few weeks he approached the students who had been so critical, and the criticism itself gave them a basis for conversation. Because of these talks, he decided to work on changing the way he related to others.

My place in Rose's diagram was interesting. I asked her why she put me closest to the boys that hung out together. But one of the other students answered for her, "Because you let them get away with more than you let the rest of us get away with." That insight was true. I know I can't be as stern as I should with defiant students, because I admire the strength they show through their defiance. I admitted to the class that this is a problem for me and promised that in the future I would try to either be tough or loose with everyone. That seemed satisfactory. Interestingly, the class seemed more concerned about equity than degree of sternness.

The other social maps were full of revelations, too. Some people showed themselves as lonely, while others thought they weren't. Some believed themselves to be part of groups that didn't acknowledge them as members. We put the maps on one of the walls and spent days talking about the issues they brought out into the open. We discussed racial and sexual groupings, individuals feeling isolated and communications among groups.

One of the students suggested that we make another kind of map, a bossing map, so we could talk about who in the class bossed whom around. Making these maps turned out to be an easy way to get a discussion about a delicate issue started. Some students showed up at the top of all the bossing maps. Others were at the bottom, always the easy victims. Several groups of students were usually grouped together on the same level, indicating that they neither bossed nor were bossed by each other, but bossed the people below them. Finally, there were three students on just about every map that were put in a category of their own—nobody bossed them and they didn't boss anybody. As one of them described herself, "I don't see a need to boss anyone, but I won't let anyone mess with me." (See the map below.)

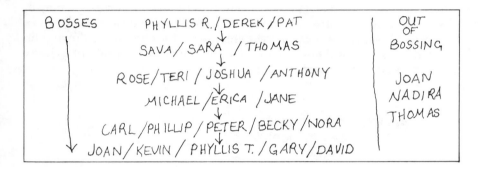

The students shared their maps, and this led to serious discussions about why some students acted so bossy and also about what it felt like to be bossed around. Some of the students brought up the point that they hung out together for mutual protection. It came out that some of the class cliques that had worried me so much were mutual protection societies, not aggressive groupings.

The discussions we had didn't immediately solve any problems in the class, but they brought important issues out into the open and got the students into the habit of discussing concerns and listening to each other. Most significantly, they helped bring about gradual positive changes.

Many of the more serious problems were settled privately and quietly. Some students began to champion the lonely and abused members of the class; surprisingly, some of the bosses became friendly with the students they abused the most. Later in the year one of the bosses told me that he was so bossy before because that was the only way he could get people to pay attention to him and be friends.

### Social Order

After we had discussed the bossing maps in class for a few days, I introduced the notion of pecking orders among animals. Thus, from the study of the social system of our classroom we moved on to look at social orders of other living creatures. First we studied chickens and looked at the way hens established an order having to do with which got first access to food and to roosters. Then we looked at dogs, and at wolf packs, prides of lions, and beehives.

In each case we made maps, and some students became very adept at devising interesting visual ways of showing social systems. One group of students did a gigantic social map of all the students in the school. As a final, last-week-of-school project, each student made a new social map of the class, and we compared these to the maps made in October. It was a nice way of seeing for ourselves the changes we felt happened during the year and of assessing how far we had come toward the goal of having a centered and harmonious class.

## 4. Metaphors Drawn from the Physical World

Sarah attracted cruelty from other children. Even the kindest child found it easy to pick on her because she cried easily and reacted to the slightest threat with panic. One day after she had been harassed at recess she exploded and just about tore the hair out of another child's head. I pulled the children apart and called the class together. Sarah's outburst had to do with all of them, not just the particular child that had provoked her to fight back.

I realized that it wouldn't do much good to simply get angry at the children who bothered Sarah as they already knew my feelings. In order to show them what had impelled her to finally break and fight back, I wanted to provide them with a physical symbol, a metaphor to internalize and use when they were tempted to bother her or some other weak child. I put on the ground the smallest of a half dozen plastic monsters that the children had been playing with. The students were surprised by my action since they had expected a lecture on Sarah. They were unusually quiet. I put another monster on the back of the first, and continued building a tower. At a certain point the monster on the bottom fell over and all the others tumbled down.

I told the children that even monsters didn't like others on their back and that at a certain point they will break down and try to throw off burdens or tormentors. My little play ended with this message: If you don't want to fall, keep off other people's backs. I hadn't praised Sarah for exploding, but I hadn't put her down for it either. What she had done was quite understandable, and while I don't like to sanction violence I am not opposed to self-defense. Most of the students got the message and left Sarah alone. She learned something, too. Realizing that she could fight back, she became less vulnerable and scared.

### Bend but Not Break

To work out the problem with Sarah, I used an image based on physical law to illustrate a principle of behavior. The reason for using physical metaphors is similar to that for using stories, fables, and tales when questions of human behavior arise. By shifting the situation away from the immediate participants you give everyone a chance to think, to withdraw from the problems and to save face. Otherwise, it is difficult to cool down emotions, avoid defensiveness or guilt and eliminate recurrences of the same problems.

I've found that there are many instances in which a metaphorical physical example can help children deal with interpersonal situations (particularly those concerned with limits) more effectively and with less embarrassment than can a direct discussion of behavior. It is important to remember though, that the physical analogy is just that—a roughly parallel image used to assist thought. There is no scientific connection between the image and the physical law, and children should understand that.

Pliability is one of many concepts that can be illustrated physically. Once, for example, some students pushed me beyond the limits of my tolerance. They were playing some computer games with a new machine and being noisier than necessary. Naturally they were excited, but I had to work with some other students on their writing. We needed the room to be reasonably quiet, and every two or three minutes I had to tell the children at the computer to keep the din down. They would quiet down for a moment, but the volume always increased again.

I accelerated my threats: "One more time and you'll have to turn off the machine," "You'll lose your turn," and so on. I don't believe in empty threats, but I realized that I really didn't want to carry them out in this instance. A number of youngsters who had been afraid of the machine were beginning to use it with confidence, and I judged that the learning that was occurring was more important than a simple application of discipline. I decided that I wanted to dramatize the point that I was reaching my tolerance limit, and yet let the students on the computer continue their work. So I called both the computer group and the writing group together to explain my feelings.

Holding up a large piece of paper, I told the children that we would consider a math problem before going on with our work. I gave the paper to one of the computer students who had been the noisiest and asked him how many times he thought he could successively fold the paper in half. He said at least a dozen, and he tried. By the eighth fold it became impossible to bend the paper another time. At this point, I gave another student a sheet of newspaper, which was twice the size of the first paper, and asked her to try the same thing. She did and the eighth fold was her last.

I told the group that, even the most pliable substance reaches a point where it won't fold anymore, no matter how large it is. My final comment was that I'd bent for the computer group at least seven times and I had just about reached my limit. The strategy worked and we got on with the writing uninterrupted.

Sometimes, different physical examples can illustrate the same concept in different ways. For example, to extend the metaphor and the notion of pliability in materials and people, examine how it varies from substance to substance and person to person. A piece of cloth or paper folds, a brittle piece of wood breaks, a rubber tube bends but never quite folds over. These variations in material are analogous to the different ways in which individuals deal with pressure or with decision making. Some people can withstand pressure for a long time before giving up. Others break easily. Still others almost never give in. By discussing character types in class you help children get a sense of how they and others react.

### Other Laws of Limitation

Other physical laws of limitation provide useful parallels to situations in which people violate the limits of sensible behavior:

*1. The Heisenberg Principle.* First proposed by the German physicist Werner Heisenberg and later verified, the Heisenberg principle states that it is impossible to exactly determine the behavior of a physical particle without affecting its motion. Simply phrased, the closer you get to observe a particle in motion, the more effect your instrument of observation has on the motion you observe.

There are many human analogies to this principle that the observer affects the behavior of the observed. For example, when your principal, parents, or an administrator comes in to view your lesson, your behavior changes and so does that of your students. I've never figured out a way to avoid the problem and make the situation more natural, but I have discussed the Heisenberg principle with observers and with my students. I have found that by understanding the effects of observation we can be a bit more relaxed and can help observers be more so, too. One observation cannot give a full impression of work in a classroom, and as the observer comes back many times he or she diminishes the Heisenberg effects by becoming more a part of the whole group.

*2. Limits of the Strength of Materials.*  Beams and columns, whether made of steel or wood, have a limit to the load they can bear. If you apply enough stress, especially at weak points, they will sag and eventually give way. You can demonstrate this vividly with simple bridges made out of balsa wood or straws. Studying the stress limits of building materials can lead to discussions of the "last straws" of students and teachers. I discuss and demonstrate this principle to explain to students why I can't meet all their needs simultaneously. I want them to understand that I have my breaking point as they do, and that we have to learn to respect each other's limits in order to get along congenially.

*3. The Limit of Simultaneity.*  A thing or person cannot be in two places at once. This truth is obvious but is not often acknowledged in the classroom. For example, when I read part of an interesting book to my students many of them want to borrow it, and they fight over it as if it is my fault that we have only one copy. Over and over again I have to explain why it is necessary to take turns with limited resources, including the teacher's time. Even though they are aware of the limits of simultaneity, they have trouble dealing with them patiently.

I've tried to help my students cope by asking them to imagine that a book or game could be in many places at once. I ask them how they would share three or four copies. We usually play around with the idea of copying books or cloning people. But we face up to the physical reality and the limits it puts on our behavior. Together we develop procedures to ensure that everyone has fair access to what is available.

### Solutions

If you are committed, as I am, to running a classroom in which children have choices, I think you'll find that physical metaphors are very useful. They provide vivid images of the limitations we have to live with and can focus group thought on the solutions to problems rather than on individual difficulties with personal behavior.

## 5. Improvisation and Self-Discipline

There are days when I simply can't keep my class together. Maybe because it's raining or something happened on the way to school. I may not even know the reasons, but I have to deal with the immediate fact that most of the children don't want to be in school that day much less do any work.

Things aren't too bad when we're involved in individual or small-group activity, but that's not all the time. Once a morning I bring the whole class together and either present a new activity or new material, continue an earlier discussion, or try to deal with some of our group problems. It is at this time that things fall apart.

There are always some students who will roll around on the floor, or hit someone, or make jokes, or try to provoke me into screaming and yelling and sending them out of the room. I find that losing my temper never helps, and sending students out of the room often results in their bothering other teachers and students. Consequently, I have developed a number of ways of turning this restlessness into something productive.

I first discovered a way to settle the class down on a day when things were so out of control that I was ready, despite my best intentions and strongest will, to grab and shake a particularly troublesome boy. I moved towards him with the most menacing look I could muster and picked him up brusquely. The clamor turned to silence, as the children waited for the hammer to fall.

I gritted my teeth, turned the student over my lap and raised my hand as if to spank him. Then I lowered my hand as slowly as possible and proceeded to mime spanking the child, whispering to him that his role was to pretend to cry. He let out incredibly drawn out and mournful moans. The other students caught on immediately, and all asked for a turn at being spanked.

After obliging a few, I asked everyone to sit down and announced that we would try something new. It would have been useless to try to go back to what I had originally planned for that day. The class sat quietly and expectantly.

I asked two of the most restless students to stand up and get ready to mock fight each other. I told them that they could not touch one another and only move in slow motion, controlling their bodies so that they never broke out of the slow rhythm of the mime. I asked one of the students to practice, and she quickly realized that it wasn't easy to slow up her body and take conscious control over her movement.

Afterwards, I asked them to mock embrace. Then I asked the whole class to stand up as slowly as they could, to raise their hands as high as possible and, when they couldn't go any higher, to get up on tiptoe and pretend that they could take off and fly.

When the exercise ended, the students fell on the rug and giggled and rolled around. After awhile they quieted down and asked for more improvisations.

I suggested that everyone lie down on their backs, close their eyes and imagine they were asleep. I told them I would be the dream master and that they would live and move in a dream for awhile. Then I said we were all under water and could only move the way fish did. I suggested they begin to swim around and think of the kind of fish they were—sharks or minnows, beautiful tropical fish, or fearsome blowfish. Although the spell was broken by a fire drill, I was amazed at the self-discipline some of the most unruly children showed.

### Taking Control

A few days later, during the dreary rainy season in northern California, things got out of hand again. I decided to go along with the students' physical restlessness and asked everyone to stand up and shout as loud as they could for 30 seconds. Then I asked them to be quiet for the same length of time. Next we ran in place and pretended to be fighting, again, for the same amount of time, and finally they pretended to walk slowly down the street, meeting friends and shaking their hands.

Now they had warmed up. It was time for more elaborate improvisations. The students mimed driving their parents' cars, picking up buildings, taking each other's pictures, flying airplanes—taking all the power of grownups.

Slowly I began to integrate the development of physical self-control into our morning rug time. Usually we spent five minutes a day at mine, slowing down or speeding up movements and developing ideas and themes through body movement, without the mediating function of words.

Things stayed that way until one day I noticed a student walk to the bookcase in slow motion, pick out a book and sit down to read it with the same mime set. When I asked what he was doing, he said that reading scared him, which was true. He threw books on the floor and would do anything to avoid having to face things that smacked of reading. He said he thought it might be because he was too fast and too angry, so he decided to see what would happen if he used mime and read slowly.

### Finding One's Own Pace

Often school is too fast for students or too slow. They are not allowed to pace themselves and are never given the idea that it is possible to come to understand and develop their own pace and style of learning. The fast learners are rewarded; the slow ones punished. And yet what difference does it make if one learns to read quickly or slowly? The quality of your ability does not depend on the speed with which you acquired the skill.

I have three children. One began to talk at 11 months, another at 18 months, the third in between. Now that they are all over five, it makes no difference in their lives or their ability to communicate.

We as teachers have to understand and support our students as they develop their own styles of learning. And we have to give them ways of slowing themselves down or speeding up if that is what they need or feel they have to do.

Body control is not divorced from mind control. As students practice controlling their bodies and learn to experiment with different paces, they also learn indirectly how to control their minds. Teachers have to learn how to make the bridge, to integrate the body and the mind. Viola Spolin's *Improvisation for the Theater* (Northwestern University Press) is a rich source of ideas for improvisations. The improvisations that worked best with my classes are the ones that involved everyone, and not those that involve a small number of students performing for the rest of the class. One of my favorite forms of improvisation (I learned it from Viola Spolin's book) consists of:

1. Sending a student or a group of students out of the room.
2. Having the class develop a dramatic situation in which the people out of the room have a central role.
3. Getting everyone in the class involved in the set situation and . . .
4. Having the students in the hall return to the room, figure out the roles they are to play, and then get involved in playing out those roles.

For example: Everyone in the room can be an animal in the forest and the students in the hall can be huntsmen; or the students in the room can be devils and the ones in the hall new arrivals in hell; or the persons in the hall can be visitors to a wax museum and the ones in the classroom dummies made of wax.

An interesting variation on this last idea developed in one of my classes. One of our students discovered that in the San Francisco Wax Museum there is an actor made up to look like a wax dummy. His job is to move when people aren't looking—thus adding a bit of mystery and a touch of the supernatural to the exhibit. In our improvisation everyone in the room was a person made up to look like a wax figure. The students chose their roles and moved only when the "visitors" were not looking.

# E
# *Crime and Punishment*

Ways to establish democratic procedures to deal with discipline problems in the classroom —guaranteed to work most but not all of the time.

*O*nce while I was working in another teacher's classroom with a group of fifth- and sixth-grade students on a biology project, two boys began to fight about using the microscope I had brought in. Each wanted to use it first. I immediately broke up the fight, as much to protect the delicate instrument as anything else. I also told the boys that they would have to wait until the next day to use the microscope. They left the classroom at recess time looking very angry.

When we came back to the room after recess we found that the microscope had been dismantled and its parts thrown all around the science center. The classroom teacher was livid. She grabbed the two boys, and accused them of breaking up the microscope. However, each boy swore that he was innocent but that he heard in the schoolyard that the other one had committed the crime. The two boys started accusing each other and almost had another fight.

Though the teacher's first reaction was to want to punish both boys, I requested time to talk to the class before any action was taken. I began by saying that whoever had broken the microscope had done harm to the whole class, not merely to the teacher or to me, and that whoever was found guilty should have to restore something to the whole class. It might be money for a new microscope, or some kind of work that would be the equivalent of the broken instrument. Since we had no definite proof of guilt, I suggested that we might be punishing an innocent person by punishing both boys. So I brought up the idea of setting up a jury trial and having the jury decide who was guilty. I have supervised student courts a number of times (only with serious offenses, since it's so time consuming) and have found that if they are handled sensitively most issues that come before them are settled justly and compassionately.

### Order in the Court

All the children were enthusiastic, especially the two angry boys. From the way the two began to talk, I could tell that they each planned on handpicking the jury, threatening the judge and generally dominating the proceedings.

In my experience I have found this thought of manipulation to be a common reaction among a group of students who are unaccustomed to self-government. In such a case it is important to have as the judge a nonpartisan adult who will be able to deal with the verdict, the recommended sentence, and possible pleas for an appeal. This safeguard will provide constraints to prevent particular students from intimidating others or taking over and running a corrupt system. There is no more reason to assume that students will automatically be righteous and fair in the administration of justice; some of their adult models have certainly provided other examples.

### The Proceedings of the Microscope Trial

In the case of the broken microscope, the jury would have a difficult job. Since two boys were on trial, either one could be declared guilty, both declared guilty or both found innocent. I asked each boy to choose a classmate as a "lawyer" to argue his case, explaining that this lawyer would question the other boy and call witnesses. The boys had no trouble deciding on lawyers. Each chose his own best buddy. This is what usually happens, and it makes the selection of a somewhat impartial jury a lot easier. The hardest job is to select a "prosecuting attorney" who will do a good, fair job gathering information and identifying witnesses to argue the case against the defendants. It is important to choose a well-respected student for this role, and in order not to isolate that student from the rest of the class, to let him or her pick a team of two other lawyers to help with the preparation of the case.

For our trial, James and Robert, the defendants, chose John and Paul, respectively, as their lawyers. As the prosecuting attorney, the teacher chose Julie, a well-liked student who is independent and very smart, and someone the other students respected. Julie chose Rachael and Judith as her assistants.

Now we were ready to begin jury selection, a proceeding which turned out to be much more complex than the students had anticipated. Each defendant was allowed six discharges, as was the prosecuting attorney. I explained that discharges were to be used to disqualify jurors (students whose names were drawn from a hat) whom it is felt might let their biases prevent them from coming to a reasoned conclusion.

I stressed that this selection process would be used in our classroom just as it is in the actual courtrooms and to make every effort to try to pick a fair, representative group of peers of the defendants rather than set up someone for an unjust verdict.

The selection of the jury was a studied, careful process. The students knew who would not be fair to whom and they knew the cliques in the classroom and who was likely to follow which group. Julie was very astute in questioning potential jurors. She had Judith make up a list of all the students and then divide them into these groups: *James's friends*; *Robert's friends*; *James's enemies*; *Robert's enemies*; *others (scared)*; *others (not scared)*.

Julie clearly attempted to eliminate as many of James' and Robert's enemies as possible or at least balance their friends with their enemies.

### The Trial Begins

We decided in advance that 8 out of 12 votes would be needed for conviction, and that any new evidence brought in would be grounds for an appeal to be settled by the teacher after a hearing. As the trial progressed both Robert and James produced witnesses who testified that they were playing with them during recess when the microscope was damaged. Both defense cases seemed very strong and they rested. Julie, however, came up with a surprise. She had two witnesses from another classroom who testified that they had seen Robert throughout the whole recess, and that they had seen James go in the school building in the middle of recess. Since these witnesses were not particularly James' enemies, they made a good impression on the jury which voted 9–3 to convict James and 12–0 to acquit Robert. James was asked if he wanted to make an appeal, but he accepted the decision and said he just wanted to get the sentencing over with.

Next, I spent time with the jury talking about the kinds of sentences they could reasonably give. We didn't want to punish James in a way that would stigmatize him; we also hoped to replace or repair the microscope. The students suggested he do some work to help pay for the microscope. One girl suggested that he do all the work to run a school dance and that the proceeds from tickets go to the microscope. However, others agreed that that was too much fun. They all finally agreed that James should hold two weekend car washes and be expected to raise $50. They said he could have his friends help him. James accepted his verdict as did most of the students. A few would really have liked to see something much worse happen, even though when pressed they couldn't tell me what those horrible punishments should be.

### Beyond the Class Trial

After the trial I brought the class a set of copies of *Inherit the Wind* by Jerome Lawrence and Robert E. Lee (Bantam), which is the story of the Scopes trial in play form. I wanted to go beyond just the class trial and relate our experience to American law and courtrooms.

Other historic trials from the trial of Socrates to that of the Watergate figures can be discussed and acted out. It is essential for students to understand our system of jury trials, and this might also be a good time to study those sections of the Constitution that discuss legal rights.

A more elaborate law curriculum might consider the rights of young people, the making and changing of laws, and the process of appeals. A visit to a courthouse and discussions with local lawyers, public defenders, legal aid groups, and prosecutors can also enrich students' understanding of law. But no matter how far you go beyond the classroom trial, it's important to deal with serious offenses at school in a democratic way that involves students in the decision making. That is, after all, what they will have to do as informed citizens. If they are not equipped to do so, we'll all suffer.

### What about the Civil Rights of a Child Being Tried?

The question of the civil rights of children in school is crucial, not merely in a situation of a mock jury trial but in any system of discipline. There are certain fundamental human rights that must be respected. Among these, in the words of the United Nations' Universal Declaration of Human Rights, is the right "in full equality to a fair and public hearing by an independent and impartial tribunal, in determination of his rights and obligations and of any criminal charge against him." I believe this should hold true of disciplinary hearings initiated by a teacher or administrator as well as of any class jury trial.

The potential for a kangaroo court threatens the very basis of democracy. Eric Partridge in *Slang To-day and Yesterday* defines "kangaroo court" as a mock court set up by prisoners in a jail to assess which possessions of a new prisoner are to be confiscated by the old prisoners and shared by them. *Webster's* defines it as "a mock court in which the principles of law and justice are disregarded or perverted." It is not a trial by jury but a trial by fiat.

In fact one of the reasons I began experimenting with jury trials was to teach students through participation the responsibilities of a legal system which presumes people innocent until proven guilty. A jury trial in a highly competitive and repressive learning environment can become a way of getting even or expressing frustration rather than of treating an accused individual justly. The possibility of a kangaroo court in such a context is real. Therefore, it is probably unwise to have a jury trial in your class unless you have been able to establish a feeling of pride and cohesiveness among students and consequently they have a high regard for each other.

If the atmosphere is wrong for a class trial, perhaps a better way to teach the nature of the jury process would be through improvisation. For example, two students could leave the room, make up an imaginary crime, then decide which of them did it and work out the details. Each of them would go on trial separately and defend themselves. Lawyers and juries could be appointed and the juries would finally decide which one was actually guilty. Since there are two trials, students can compare them and see how the deliberations of the two juries differed.

In any case, it is probably inadvisable to use a jury trial for every offense in school. The technique is only one possible means of settling problems. The reason I experimented with that form was that I, as a recent juror impressed by how concerned and intelligent our very diverse jury was over its charge, wanted to share my participation in the democratic process with my students. Though there were diverse personalities in the group of students, there was mutual respect and I felt that with proper guidance they could reach as fair a verdict as possible.

### What Guarantee Does One Have That a Trial Will Be Fair?

Several safeguards that are built into our legal processes should guarantee fairness to a class court as much as to a real court. One is the defendant's (or his or her lawyer's) right to challenge any juror who seems to be biased. In that way one tries to seat the fairest possible jury.

In rethinking the topic, I believe that another safeguard is never to put any child on trial in the classroom unless he or she voluntarily agrees to it. And the child should not be put in a position of agreeing because of a fear of consequent rejection by other students or the teacher.

A trial should not be (and I didn't mean to suggest that it should) the sole way of dealing with discipline or theft or violence in the classroom. There may be some students who do not want to go before their peers and others who intimidate their peers and therefore will never be convicted. A teacher has to use discretion in deciding when a particular form of authority is appropriate.

I know I may be opening myself up to criticism again, but I don't believe that one should take a rigid punitive approach to discipline in school. I think students' motivation for nonsocial behavior has to be understood. For example, I don't believe it's possible to eliminate violence simply by punishing offenders. It is important to get at the root source of the violence. Or, take a lesser crime. I know of a school where students caught smoking or writing on walls are taken out of class and made to sit in the office. A child in that school told me that the students who do most of the smoking and writing on walls do it to get out of classes.

I feel that it's important in these times when people talk about wanting a return to basics and stronger discipline to remember that strict authoritative punishment has never really worked.

### Did the Child's Parents Agree with the Trial?

In the case of my own experiments with jury trials in the classroom, I did not ask for formal permission to conduct trials. I spoke to the parents of my students informally and explained that on a temporary basis, as part of a unit on the citizen and democracy, I would hold several trials. I also knew my students and their parents well. Depending on your situation, it may be advisable to get parents to sign formal permission notes before proceeding. You should definitely make it clear to them exactly what you are doing.

I believe that all methods of discipline should be explained to parents, and that parents ultimately should have the last word about whether their children are to be subjected to a certain system of control or not. Once one of my own children's teachers used a system of control that was morally objectionable to me. I spoke to the teacher about it, and we had to negotiate a mutually acceptable way to deal with unacceptable behavior. That process of negotiation with prime regard for the rights of the individual is also part of the nature of democracy. It is all too easy for a person in authority to forget that the power he or she has should be used for the benefit of those it is intended to serve.

### Did the Child's Parents Agree to Abide by the Verdict?

The parents of the children in my class understood what I was doing, understood the safeguards and did agree. Nevertheless, given our human finiteness, the chance that we might be mistaken and an innocent person found guilty always exists under any system of discipline. That is why there is an appeal process in the courts and that is why there should be one in school—no matter what the form of authority.

In addition it is important to remember that in our system of justice the jury pronounces the verdict and the judge imposes the sentence. There are hanging judges and compassionate judges. I do not believe that educators should act like hanging judges. In most class trials I have been involved with in which the defendant was found guilty, the trial itself was sentence enough for the child. The sentence usually involved promising not to do the thing again or promising to do some useful work that would help others.

The first time a class of mine used a trial, one of the children had destroyed another's watch. After the trial, which was noisy but compassionate, the students suggested a sentence that seemed just and sensible to me. They recommended that the child who broke the watch wash cars and do other errands to work off the price of replacing the watch. They also suggested that she be given a year to do it. This sentence put an end to the situation. The child who had broken the watch was paying off a debt, and when that was done there was no question of anyone having to get even with her or for her to have to bear abiding guilt.

I am convinced that whether one has an occasional real trial in the classroom or sets up an improvised one, the working knowledge of what it is like to be in a courtroom and on a jury is vital for all of our children.

# F
# Uniqueness and Cooperation

A series of units that help students understand
their uniqueness and special place in the world
and that show them the strength in cooperation
at the same time.

*S*tarting with the East African concept of cooperation called *ujima* in Swahili, students can learn to get along with one another better and to minimize competition while continuing to appreciate their own uniqueness.

### 1. Ujima
### — Let's All
### Pull Together

I was involved in the development of a game learning center at one of the primary schools in Berkeley. Students in the center were encouraged to teach each other games they knew and help each other develop interesting play strategies. The emphasis was on mutual problem solving and collective learning rather than on competitive gaming.

At the beginning of the year there was only one student, a third grader, who knew how to play chess. He attended the center with three other third graders and four second graders. When I encouraged him to teach the others to play, he refused saying that he didn't want to teach someone else how to beat him.

After a while, however, he relented and showed two girls the wrong moves. Until I stopped him, he took pleasure in beating them all the time. The way he taught the game guaranteed that he would win easily.

The situation was paradoxical. On the one hand, he often complained that he had no one around with whom he could play an interesting game of chess. At the same time, he didn't want to share his knowledge of the game because he was afraid of losing the competitive advantage he had. I was initially furious at him but, after a while, realized that what he was doing in the game center was what most students are taught to do in all subjects in their regular classrooms.

To know more than someone else is to have a competitive advantage over other students. It is also often taken as a sign that one is better, more intelligent, superior to others. Knowledge is something to be shared, a gift that one person has that can be used to benefit everyone. Rather, in many schools it is considered a token that distinguishes the individual student from the rest of the herd and, therefore, is a commodity that must be hoarded and protected.

I find such a competitive attitude destructive in the classroom as well as in adult life. One of my goals in working with children is to develop a sense of community in the group. Knowledge in that context is something to share as a matter of course, and as much pleasure is to be had from sharing and teaching someone else what you know as from learning something yourself. Over the years I have been trying to translate that lofty sounding goal into everyday classroom practice. Here's an example of one approach to cooperation that I tried when teaching a combined kindergarten-first grade. The same materials and concepts could easily be adapted to any elementary grade level.

The issue of cooperation naturally arises in the context of studying a country that views cooperative living as essental to its way of life. I chose Tanzania as an instance of a cooperative society worth studying because it fit with my desire to develop multicultural perspectives in the students and because cooperation, *ujima*, is central to its self-definition as a nation. We began our study of Tanzania by looking at a map.

Recently we have been introducing our class of first graders and kindergarteners to East Africa. We have looked at maps of the world and taken imaginary journeys from Berkeley to Dar-es-Salaam, the capital. Then the students learned simple greeting in Swahili, such as *jambo* (hello), *kwa Heri* (good bye), and *asante* (thank you).

I introduced the concept of ujima by writing the words "ujima" and "cooperation" on the chalkboard. Then I handed out cards to a group of children. One of the letters of those two words was printed on each card. I asked the students to spell out the words by arranging themselves in the right order.

At first the students asked me who had the "u," who had the "j" and so on. I refused to answer and encouraged them to organize themselves. After awhile they were able to spell out the words, and I explained that the process of getting together was ujima.

The next day I brought a number of simple jigsaw puzzles to school and gave each child a piece (we did this in groups of ten). Then I asked them if, using ujima, they could put the puzzles together. They succeeded eventually in deciding who would put the first piece down. They looked at each other's pieces, decided on a strategy to follow and after awhile assembled the puzzles.

Next I brought in an 81-piece puzzle that none of the students could assemble by themselves. However, when they sat down in a group with an adult to guide them a bit they succeeded. The group could solve the task that no individual could master.

### Ujima and Learning

I pointed out to the class that the same thing could happen in reading and math. There are some children in the class who already read quite well and some who barely know the alphabet, while the knowledge needed for *everyone* to learn is already there, the tendency is for those who know to put down those who don't. If the class would use ujima, everyone would move along more quickly.

There are some ways in which this is beginning to happen. The students are sharing their solutions to problems in their math work-books. We try to discourage sharing that is merely copying someone else's answer. We become excited when groups of students solve problems together. That is now happening quite often.

A new boy recently joined the class, and several of the older children insisted I give him a math workbook, which they showed him how to use. For a week they worked with him until he caught up to them, and they could move on together.

One day I challenged five of the children to a tug of war. I won. Then ten more students joined in and by using ujima they beat me.

During group time we discussed many different instances of ujima, such as when one student mediated a fight between two others or when one of the girls helped another climb the bars. The playground has been a fertile area for introducing the students to ujima.

There used to be continual fights over who was to bat first, and who was out. I introduced a new rule to the game, teams were to be penalized by getting an out for lack of ujima. The first day we tried it, one of the students refused to accept the fact that he had struck out, wouldn't give the bat to the next batter and started cursing a bit. I called one out, two outs, before the third out was called for lack of ujima, the problem ended. After awhile there are not too many ujima outs.

The lunchroom is another spot of ujima. I refused to assign the children numbers, which would force them to line up in a set way. The first in line each day is chosen according to alphabetical progression. The rest of the students are expected to line up in a congenial way, without struggling over places. One day in frustration over the struggle for position in line, I sat the class down and asked whether lunch tasted better if they were first in line. After awhile the issue of first and last seemed less important.

Things don't change instantly. It requires patience and persistence to develop cooperation among young people who are surrounded by a higher competitive world of adults.

Another way we have been introducing the idea of cooperation is through tales and legends. The story of Anansi the spider and his six sons, for example, shows how all the sons, by using their different skills, save their father (which no one of them could have done alone). *Anansi the Spider: A Tale from Ashanti*, adapted and illustrated by Gerald McDermott (Holt, Rinehart, and Winston, 1972).

Other stories can be found in Julius Lester's *Black Folktales* (Grove Press, 1967). Many of these tales tell of the tragic consequences resulting from a lack of cooperation rather than the positive virtues of collective action.

### Why Ujima?

One question might arise. Why use the word ujima at all? Isn't cooperation adequate? Perhaps it is, but I find that students are up to their eyes in admonitions about cooperation, and a new word makes it possible for them to develop a more complex image of collective work and mutual respect.

Besides, as the word "cooperation" is generally used in the classroom, it means doing what the teacher wants you to do. Ujima refocuses the issue and enables the students to look at how they function with each other and what they can do as individuals to make a coherent and congenial whole in their own classroom and hopefully in their own lives as well.

### 2. Listening to Each Other

The quality of students' relationships with each other is certainly as important as is their relationship with their teacher. I have found that learning can take place with greater ease and in greater depth in classrooms where students are kind to each other and respect classmates' opinions than in rooms where students constantly put each other down and court the teacher. For that reason it is worth spending time during the first few weeks of school to establish a cooperative tone. Through experimentation I've discovered and developed a number of approaches to help students become accustomed to listening to and assisting each other.

Several summers ago at the Coastal Ridge Research and Education Center Summer School in California, I combined two of these techniques and felt it helped a great deal in cementing positive relationships among the students. The first technique, which my students found extremely interesting, is an adaptation of the "Olympic Game," devised by the Development Education Staff of the Toronto Miles for Millions program. The Olympic Game, designed to assist students in understanding cultural differences among people, was set in Canada (host country for the 1976 Olympics). Using my adaptation, we pretended to host a Young People's Olympics.

### The Olympic Game

First I divided my class of 30 students into three groups of ten. Members of the first group, the observers, weren't told anything. They were to sit together, watch the game, and then try to describe what was happening. They had to figure out the setting and the roles that the members of the other groups played.

I told members of the second group that they would play the roles of Californians who were hosting a party for visiting youth-Olympians from several different imaginary countries. They were to describe California and make their guests feel at home. I provided fruit juice and cookies and some crepe paper and felt-tipped markers so they could create a party-like atmosphere.

The ten children in the third group split up into pairs to play visiting Olympians from each of the following imaginary countries: Zhabori, Valdesta, Montza, Syrabia, and Flavint. (The first four countries were in the original game and I invented Flavint). I explained that each of the countries has different party manners and gave each pair of students a description of the manners of their country and some time to rehearse those manners.

I told the students that in Zhabori it is not polite to look directly at people while talking to them. Therefore, during the party the only polite way to behave towards your hosts is never to look at them. In Valdesta, things are quite different. To be friendly and polite you must stand very close to other people so that your faces are almost touching. In Montza, politeness takes still another form. To show appreciation for your hosts you are supposed to touch them and hold their hands while you are talking to them. In Syrabia, no one ever responds to a question or statement without pausing for a while in order to show that the hosts' remarks are being taken seriously. Finally, in Flavint, politeness is considered a sign of weakness and submission, and hosts are accustomed to being insulted by their guests. When I had finished explaining their roles to groups two and three, and they'd had time to get ready, the party began.

### No Right or Wrong

Though the students were shy about getting into their roles at first, the juice and cookies helped get things started. The hosts were bewildered by the different styles of behavior of their guests and struggled to maintain their poise. The observers quickly realized that there was a party for athletes of different countries going on, but were also puzzled about the varying behaviors. Soon, however, the observers began to notice patterns, and a member of the team suggested that they chart the behavior of students from different countries. Some wanted to rank the countries from best to worst, but they soon realized that though they could easily find the differences, they had no basis for determining the worth of the different systems of conduct.

The observers said that the improvisation forced them to forget their usual way of looking at their classmates. I noticed that some students who were known for behaving outrageously on occasion forgot their usual class roles and became absorbed in observing and acting.

After the improvisation, which lasted about ten minutes, we discussed what had happened. This analysis was as important in helping achieve my goals for my students as was the improvisation itself. During the analysis the actors described what it felt like working into their roles. Some of the hosts said they had just decided to imitate their guests; others had refused to compromise and had stuck to their "California" behavior. Generally, the guests felt their most awkward moment was the first attempt at being polite.

We talked for about half an hour, and then the students decided to make up their own improvisation and try it out the next day. In it the students divided themselves into groups (five students each) representing six countries, set behavioral rules for themselves, and met at the "United Nations" to settle a boundary dispute between two of the countries. The students in the other four countries were to decide whether to be neutral or take sides as the debate developed.

Throughout both of these improvisations I noticed that no student was left out of the process of stood out as better or worse than anyone else. These nonjudgmental improvisations created a group cohesiveness that carried over to the playground and to the students' willingness to help each other with academic work.

### Life Patterns

To follow up the improvisations, I used a technique for describing the rhythm of people's lives that my daughter Erica had developed a few months before. On the way home from a family trip, we had stopped at a restaurant where we had seen a woman who seemed very depressed. My oldest daughter Antonia said she reminded her of a friend of ours who had committed suicide and wondered how she could have felt bad enough to kill herself. I tried to describe my impression of our friend's life and found myself talking more with my hands than I usually do.

My friend's life had been full of major ups and downs and I must have moved my hands in a way that suggested a sine curve. Erica immediately said her life was like a different curve. She explained with this graph.

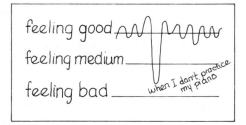

Then we all picked up on Erica's ideas and throughout dinner we graphed our lives and the lives of our friends.

As I introduced Erica's technique to my students this summer, I told them that there is no correct way to live or feel; that the rhythm of life changes over time, and that sharing graphs is one way of telling people about yourself and of coming to understand them as well. I stressed that anyone who felt uncomfortable doing a graph didn't have to. In this particular group all the students did draw graphs and I noticed that they paid very close attention to each other's work. Some indicated that the pattern of their lives was similar to the graph on page 216.

As students shared graphs, other people in the class asked them what set off swings from good to bad, and what people did when they felt bad or what they did to make themselves keep calm. I noticed that after sharing thoughts about their own lives with each other, this particular group of students seemed kinder to each other than many I have worked with.

good _____
medium _____
bad _____


good _____
medium _____
bad _____


good _____
medium _____
bad _____

### To Understand Differences

These two simple exercises got my students talking to each other and trying to understand differences among themselves and others. I believe that the development of mutual respect was begun, and I hope they continue to nurture it.

## 3. Being Unique

One summer I put on the play *Antigone* with a group of third through seventh graders. I wrote an elaborate battle scene for the eight boys who chose to play the Greek warriors. Because I had taken fencing in college, I could show the students a variety of thrusts and parries to enable them to look fierce and impressive on stage. A friend of mine made nice clanging swords for the boys out of hollow aluminum rods and plywood. She gave each sword a rubber tip for safety.

After each practice I collected the swords for storage in our costume room. At the third practice, when I began passing out the swords, an interesting thing happened. Robert immediately complained that I had given him the wrong sword. My son, Josh, who received the next sword, did the same thing. I laughed at the boys and told them that the swords were all alike. I had asked my friend to make sure that each sword was the same length and that each hand guard was the same shape to be sure no one would think his sword was either better or worse than the others. The boys said I was wrong. Robert told me that his sword had a knot on the hand guard next to the blade, and Josh said that his sword had gotten a dent on it when Charles had hit it out of his hand during the last practice.

I then asked the other boys if they could tell their own swords. Sure enough, each of the eight swords I had seen as identical was unique in the eyes of the children.

At the beginning of this school year I witnessed a similar incident in a friend's classroom. With the help of a hobbyist parent, his students had rubber molds to cast British and American Revolutionary War lead soldiers. The lead was obtained from fishing weights. Each student had made six soldiers and used hobby enamel to paint them according to the directions.

Before the students got the chance to take their soldiers home, they had gotten mixed up. They all looked alike to the parent so he randomly labeled them with the names of the students in the class. The day I was there the students had come to get their soldiers. There was an immediate uproar. Students complained that the soldiers with their names on them were not the ones they had painted. Moreover, they could explain in detail what made their own soldiers unique.

Each child had given his or her own work a touch that somehow made it unique. Sometimes the identifying mark was negative. One boy, for example, said that the soldiers he was given were too well painted. He said he had messed up the paint job. A girl said that she had given all her soldiers green and yellow socks even though she knew that those colors weren't really a part of the soldiers' historic costumes.

These two instances gave me a strong reminder of how important uniqueness is in education. I have seen that some of the most important learning takes place when the learner expresses something that is uniquely his or hers. Making room for the divergence of the children's expression gives character and depth to learning. It's such individuality that helps children gain self-respect and dignity in the eyes of others. Differences don't have to lead to hierarchies of people labeled superior or inferior.

Involved in the everyday grind of teaching, grading and working, teachers and students can easily forget these seemingly obvious truths. Students often ridicule failure and ineptitude when they could be helping their classmates instead. Teachers do the same thing in more subtle ways.

It's also important to have in mind that though it is difficult for students to express themselves through true-false tests or learning tasks oriented toward behavioral objectives, there are many ways to open up the curriculum to uniqueness. Handwriting, for example, is one area where students define themselves. Everyone tries to develop a signature that is uniquely his or hers and a handwriting style (despite the greatest efforts of penmanship programs) that their friends will be able to identify.

An exercise I love to do with children who are learning to write (young printers and older cursive writers) is to ask each one to hand-write a paragraph so distinctively that classmates will be able to tell who did it. It can be a simple paragraph, such as: "I write fancy in my own way. You can tell my writing by the way I turn my pen."

In school we often forget that there are many ways to write legibly. There is nothing wrong with variation as long as a script can be read. In fact, variation is probably inevitable. Handwriters' rhythms and the pressure each applied to the paper differ. Rather than denying our own and our students' displays of uniqueness as they slip into our work, acknowledging and, in fact, honoring them can build confidence and pride.

## Uniqueness Activities

Here are four other activities I have used to get students to express themselves in unique ways and recognize what is individualistic about their classmates' work.

1. Draw pictures of the lines on the palms of students' hands and compare the different patterns that emerge. Or compare fingerprints made with a rubber stamp pad. It isn't necessary to believe in palmistry to find interesting the wide variations in lines and patterns interesting.

2. Put a number of shapes on the chalkboard (say two triangles, a square, a circle, a rectangle and an oval). Then ask the class to copy and arrange these forms on a sheet of paper in any way they find appealing. Compare the arrangements that emerge. Some students will cluster the forms and others will spread them out; some will arrange them symmetrically and others will prefer a random design. Comparing the various organizations of the shapes can lead to discussing the different ways in which people organize their experiences and reveal some of the range and variety of human thinking styles.

3. Arrange to observe a litter of kittens, especially one in which the newborn closely resemble each other. Look for aspects of style and

behavior that distinguish the kittens from each other. Watching a litter over a few months can lead to a sense of the emergence of personality since animals, no less than people, have traits that make them unique members of their species.

4. Many other aspects of people are unique. Voice, style of movement, profile, footprint, sense of humor, and so on. Students can learn to recognize each other's special characteristics by playing guessing games.

One game begins with having every child in the class read the same sentence or paragraph, which you have selected beforehand, into a tape recorder. Then, the tape is played and everyone guesses who is reading. Next, have students consciously disguise their voices when they read. Now try the guessing again. You'll find that even the most cleverly disguised voice usually reveals itself.

Prepare for another good guessing game by hanging a sheet across a part of the room, putting a lamp with a 250-watt bulb behind the sheet, closing the windows and turning out all the lights. Have a group of students go behind the sheet and, one at a time, walk past the light so that a shadow is projected through the sheet. The other children guess who it is and then discuss what it is that makes that person identifiable.

### What is Special About Your Work

Finally, it is worth taking some time to consider what is unique about your own work and even putting it in writing. Teachers who care about their profession do lots of special things. The reflection process will help you nurture that individuality and build on it. Your students will remember what is unique about you, not what is mechanical or stereotyped.

At this time there is pressure on many of us in public education to objectify our work and conform to mechanical teaching systems. I believe we have to reaffirm our individuality and remember that what is special about us is what will enable our students to be special too.

## 4. Shared Victory

Ron Jones is recreation director of the San Francisco Recreation Center for the Handicapped. Over the past 15 years he has been a high school English teacher, a basketball coach, the founder and central moving force in the Zephyros Education Exchange (a nonprofit collaborative of San Francisco teachers, parents, and kids), and the author of several books and some of the most interesting curriculum material I have ever seen. He has a special kind of craziness that children love.

Three summers ago, I asked Ron if he would teach at our center's summer school for eight- to 12-year-olds. Even though he didn't have much experience teaching younger children, there was no question in my mind that he'd be successful at it. Ron said he'd like to be our physical education teacher if he could try out some games and events that he might be able to use with the adults he worked with during the year. I agreed, thinking of the parallel between Ron, who worked with handicapped adults experimenting with our students, and Maria Montessori, who worked first with retarded adults and then used her methods as the basis for her system for nonretarded children.

### Crazy Fun

Ron's basic idea was to provide fun in a structured and challenging physical way through crazy, noncompetitive contests. One of his inspirations must have been the *Guiness Book of World Records* (by Norris McWhirter and Ross McWhirter, Sterling), since each contest had the potential of creating an intriguing new world's record. These contests accomplish little more than providing pleasure and a bit of illumination of different subject areas. However, they do create a pause from the pressure of everyday life in school and become occasions for students and teachers to talk and play together. They also provide opportunities for people to discover unexpected strengths in each other. For me one of the most interesting aspects of developing Ron's "unusual world records" was that students who did least well in most traditional school subjects were the most inventive and active participants in all of our silly events.

Ron's materials consisted of several inner tubes and miscellaneous cans, boxes, and pipes that he found around our place. In addition to designing each event and game to be noncompetitive he made sure each was fun to observe and participate in. One of the contests Ron tried with my students (and ended up using with his students at the Recreation Center for the Handicapped) was "Most People Standing on an Inner Tube." Here's how he describes the event in his marvelous new book, *Share Victory* (published by Ron Jones, 1201 Stanyan St., San Francisco, CA 94117, $4.50). The book details the events Ron dreamed up and includes pictures of people at the Center for the Handicapped participating in them.

Have you even stood on an inner tube? It's not easy. You push down with one foot and the air in the tube rushes around to push up your other foot. You push harder and the washing motion of air returns the favor. You giggle and it giggles. When a friend stands on the tube with you, the air currents go every which way. And when three people try to stand on an inner tube, the only way to stay in balance is to hold on to each other and "ride out" the wiggling surface. The more people added to this ring of air, the more tides are created. Feel with your feet. Bend your legs. Hold on to your neighbor. Don't pull each other over. Hold on, that's the secret.

The current World Record for People Standing on an Inner Tube is 15. Of course, part of this record is based on finding a large inner tube. And then some friends willing to dance on rubber.

### Tallest, Largest, Most

Some of Ron's other records are:

The tallest paper cup and plate tower made by placing a paper cup on a paper plate and then building up a tower of plate, cup, plate, cup, and so on.

The largest pinball machine made out of boxes and cans and other readily available objects.

The most tennis balls stuffed in a T shirt.

The most hats worn by one person at the same time.

The most inner tubes lifted by a group.

One of my students who had played in Ron's "share victory" games and contests suggested that during the next school year we set up a class book of world records. In keeping with the spirit of his shared victories we decided to include only events no one had ever tried before (to ensure we'd have world records) and to keep the events silly so that students wouldn't get too competitive and cruel. Finally, we agreed that each person or group could only hold one world record. There would be a record for each person, and one for every group that was ingenious enough to organize its own event.

Of course, we couldn't eliminate all competition. Some groups tried to beat other groups' records, and some students tried to outdo every individual record set. But fortunately everyone did everything in such a spirit of fun that setting records didn't really matter much.

### Tapping and Hopping

Thomas suggested the first event, foot tapping. Throughout his school career Thomas had irritated classmates and teachers by tapping his foot on the floor. This time everyone had to wait and watch as he tapped away for over a half an hour, the world record.

Some other events we invented were:

The longest column of figures added up, not counting ones.
The longest flight of a paper airplane. (The students didn't know that this had been tried before.)
The shortest complete sentence. (Go!)
The longest sentence. (It's too long and convoluted to reproduce but everyone read it.)
The highest stack of books.
The longest stand on one foot.
The loudest scream.
The softest whisper. (These last two events were judgment events. We had to vote to determine winners because we couldn't figure out an objective way.)
The longest walk on hands.
The most hops in two minutes. (This was quite a difficult event to judge.)
The longest word you can find in the dictionary.

I had expected that most events would be physical. Surprisingly, the students chose many that had to do with school subjects. In fact, when they were through, I started making up silly records for every subject area. In science I thought of the following:

The smallest amoeba or paramecium seen under a microscope (How do you tell?)
The largest ant found by a student.
The largest number of different colors observed on an animal. (One student cited a cat; another said his sister had more colors on her favorite dress.)
The largest egg brought to class.
The biggest seed.

# V
# Sustaining a Life of Teaching

# A
# Sources of Renewal

On ways of building your strength when trying to teach well wears you down.

*D*uring the last year I have been traveling around the country talking to teachers and teacher groups and visiting classrooms. My observations have led me to reach two seemingly contradictory conclusions: first, many teachers are tired and demoralized and, second, despite this mood there is more creative teaching going on than there has been in years. This apparent paradox can be explained by examining the current social and economic role of the teacher.

In many school districts teachers have been laid off despite tenure laws, budgets have been tightened, and the teaching profession has been under attack in response to the pressure of inflation rather than to any particular educational issue. Given these sources of anxiety, many teachers are turning to the classroom and the specifics of teaching for release. It seems that teaching, direct work with children, is often the only source of pleasure the job provides these days. As one Midwestern teacher put it, "My salary doesn't keep up with inflation. The papers and magazines blame me for everything negative that happens. I don't know whether I'll still have a job next year or whether I'll be shifted around somewhere in the district. If I can't have some pleasure in the classroom and take some risks to teach, well, I might as well quit and drive a cab or something."

Interestingly, the risks teachers tell me they are taking in order to teach well, cluster about certain aspects of classroom life that I am now finding central in my own work. These are: spending more time talking with one's students, developing humor in the classroom, experimenting with slowing down the pace of life and thinking about self-sufficiency. I want to examine each of these and consider how they can lead to renewed energy and interest in the classroom.

### Talking with Students

Many teachers have told me they feel trapped by overly structured learning programs. They say that such programs require them to spend so much time filling out forms and testing that they have little opportunity to explain and discuss things with their students. One teacher mentioned that he was even afraid to take time to talk over a story or a current issue with his students because he felt the pressure of constantly moving through a detailed district program. He knows that no learning can occur without thought and dialogue, and he was thinking of "stealing" 15 minutes a day to talk to his students and get to know them better.

It's impossible to know your students unless they have the chance to speak out in their own voices, rather than becoming part of a stimulus-response learning system. I have been struck by how resistant students become to learning anything new after they have been conditioned by developmental learning programs. Time spent talking about almost anything of interest can create an intimacy and ease in the classroom that makes it possible to introduce new and unfamiliar material. I make a point of bringing up and discussing something unfamiliar every few days. Here are a few simple examples:

> The ingredients listed on the back of a can.
> An old photo brought in by one of the students or by the teacher.
> Some local ghost stories and stories about haunted places.
> Old proverbs that contradict each other like "Too many cooks spoil the broth" and "The more the merrier."
> A story or local legend about heroes, and bandits and lovers.
> Some curious fact about a natural phenomena or disaster.

Just about anything will do to start and open-ended conversation. Learning to speak in a group is not, as many teachers fear, just talking. It is a way of binding people together, of learning to think through an issue with the help of others and of learning to enjoy the voices, thoughts, and presence of others.

### Developing Humor
### in the Classroom

A teacher I met recently told me that if she couldn't laugh at least once a day with her students she would go crazy. Humor is an essential component of any kind of life; when it is absent tensions can become magnified and thought inhibited. However, it is impossible to legislate humor, and not everybody tells a good story or joke. One way I've been successful at adding some humor to my classroom is to tell stories about my own childhood. Students seem to find the foibles and failures of adults they know amusing no matter how awkwardly they are presented.

I've found that it's crucial that classroom humor not make fun of any other specific person or group. Amusing stories work well when they are at the expense of the teller or of some mythical character, such as Jack in the "Southern Jack" tales or people from Chelm in some Yiddish tales. Jews should only tell Jewish stories: Italians, Italian jokes. Humor is respectful when the joke is on oneself, but can be offensive and aggressive if told about others. So in the classroom it's important to be sensitive enough not to tell "children" jokes or jokes that would offend the families of the students.

Classroom humor isn't all jokes, of course. It also has to do with a lightness of touch: with the ability to see things as funny rather than defiant or all wrong. For example, it's funny, in a way, that so many students reverse letters when they are just learning to read. It's also amusing to watch two youngsters square off to fight and take on the poses of professional fighters or karate experts. With a certain wry stance I've found it possible to relax classroom tensions and joke away many so-called discipline problems.

### Slowing down the Pace

We all need ways to slow down our lives and learn to relax, especially with the continuing stress of today's social and economic uncertainties. Simple ways to relax include closing one's eyes and counting to push away all thoughts. This kind of relaxation has helped me keep from becoming too exhausted and disoriented when I travel. It has also helped me develop quiet times with students. Often, I ask everyone to get comfortable and to relax their bodies slowly from their toes on up and breathe deeply, consciously and slowly. After a few minutes of relaxation, we seem to be able to talk things out more sensibly and less emotionally.

Another slowing down system I've used for myself and with my students is to periodically take the time to list things I enjoy doing for their own sake rather than for some external reward. When my list gets small, I know it is time to think more about what is essential to me so that I won't let myself be swept away by current needs and responsibilities. I suggest that my students do the same.

Sometimes our "doing for fun" lists include ordinary or seemingly unimportant things. The last time I made a list of what I love to do for its own sake, I put down "growing tomatoes." I don't know why that activity is currently important to me, though it does have something to do with a feeling I now have of needing to grow things. Those ordinary, or even silly, things we love to do are often what makes the rest of the struggle worthwhile, and what can keep us going in times of stress or crisis.

### Thinking about Self-Sufficiency

As inflation continues, the issue of self-sufficiency become more and more central to our lives. For example, how much can we provide for ourselves and our communities by working together rather than buying separately? In schools this issue manifests itself in a number of ways. As school budgets are cut and supplies become more expensive, how can teachers and students provide themselves with adequate books and supplies? Can schools print some of their own books? Make their own paper? Grow their own food? Hook into their own solar energy systems?

These ideas are not remote. In the '20s and '30s there were schools that did manufacture their own equipment and print their own books (under what was then called the Gary Plan). In England at the same time, many schools made all the paper that was used by their students. During World War II some schools maintained "victory gardens" and did produce a substantial part of their own food. Now a number of schools are experimenting with solar energy.

There are things we can and might have to do to help ourselves, and in the course of helping ourselves we might get to know each other better. The subject of self-sufficiency is one that can be studied in science, social studies, language arts, and math. It might even be possible to make the subject the center of several multidisciplinary curriculum units. In the next articles I will make some practical suggestions about how self-sufficiency can be studied and acted upon in the classroom.

# B
# Dealing With Behavioral Objectives

Ways of using behavioral objectives to fit into,
rather than change, your way of teaching.

*A*ttempts at renewal and the creation of an interesting learning environment are often thwarted by silly and time-consuming administrative demands. The imposition of behavioral objectives is one such time-consuming, wasteful requirement that takes us teachers away from important work with our students. Yet even behavioral objectives can be turned to uses that can help rather than paralyze our work. I remember talking with a friend who teaches fourth grade about planning for the school year. The year before had started out well for her, but in December the administration in her district directed that everyone teach using a complicated group of behavioral objectives that had been developed by the central office. Reading and math were broken down into six levels with 60 objectives for each level. Teachers were expected to fill out weekly reports, which recorded each student's progress through these objectives. Tests were provided for each objective.

Towards the end of the year, my friend calculated that she was spending ten minutes testing and filling out forms for every two and a half minutes she was teaching. In mentioning this to her principal, she lamented the problems of being overwhelmed by paperwork and of behavioral objectives that break down so complexly that the flow and content and joy of reading are lost in an obsession with teaching particular and isolated skills.

She also brought up the point that her students had been doing well in reading with her old methods and that she felt her whole approach to teaching had now been undermined. Although he was sympathetic, the principal told her that all teachers had to comply with the directive. By June she had become more and more discouraged and finally was considering quitting.

At the time of our discussion, my friend told me that over the summer she had decided she had to ignore the demands of the administration and principal and teach her way, even it it meant being fired. I suggested that there was another option open to her. She could accept the notion of developing behavioral objectives for part of one's work, articulate objectives that supported that work rather than undermined it, and stand up to the administration for those personally developed goals. Next we talked about how to implement such an approach.

Whether you are searching for a solution to a situation similar to my friend's or would simply like to come to terms with the idea of behavioral objectives and their possible positive uses in your classroom, I think you might find it helpful to know how we defined the term in relation to our own teaching.

We recognized that written behavioral objectives are statements about what one wants to see happen with students, and that a teacher, administrator, or the students themselves should have a way of knowing whether or not these goals have been achieved. Then we clarified for ourselves the idea that all teaching goals cannot be translated into simple short-range behavioral terms.

If major goals of a teacher's work are to enable students to live healthy and rewarding lives as adults, to be able to relate to other people without exploiting them, and to become caring parents themselves, obviously there is no way these objectives can be evaluated in the course of one school year. Perhaps these goals can be validated in terms of behavior over a period of 30 or 40 years, but in that perspective it seems almost impossible to be certain what have been the crucial influences on people's behavior. This is no reason, however, to give up on these long-range objectives, which for me lie at the heart of teaching and are the central motivation for working so hard under what are often extremely difficult circumstances.

### Goals for a Teaching Year

As we pinned down what behavioral objectives are (in a way similar to the writing objectives in Part II) we were able to distinguish the important long-term goal from goals for a teaching year that can be looked at over short time periods. I suggested to my friend that she articulate what she wanted to happen in her classroom during the coming year and describe how she felt people could find out whether or not it happened. She could then put those ideas into the form of behavioral objectives and would be in a strong position to suggest that her own system of objectives, which relates to the best in her work, replace the set that was undermining it. This way, if a struggle were to develop, her teaching could continue to grow in the ways she had already found to be successful.

In order to begin, I suggested we ask the following questions: What would I like to see happen? How can I tell it is achieved? How can my students tell? How can others tell? (See the form on page 233.)

| Personally Developed Behavioral Objectives | | | |
|---|---|---|---|
| WHAT WOULD I LIKE TO SEE HAPPEN? | HOW CAN I TELL IT IS ACHIEVED? | HOW CAN MY STUDENTS TELL? | HOW CAN OTHERS TELL? |
| First week of school, I need to find out what students know of reading, including what they know of street words and ads, what books they seem interested in. | Fill out a reading profile (see below) on each student. | Spend a day explaining profile to them and showing them the one I do for them. | Explain profile to parents and principal. |
| Have students master compound words such as *underground, inside, uptown,* etc. | Ask students to read a book like *Upside Down and Inside Out* by *Bobbi Katz (Watts)* or play word games with compound words. | Try to read a list of compound words. | Ask students to read list, play game or read book. |

I have found it best to start with overall objectives in planning a program. With reading, for example, the question would not be what skills you want your students to acquire but rather what kinds of books and other written material you want them to be able to read and understand. Using this approach, the skills needed to deal with the material can emerge out of the material itself.

It has been my experience that many students learn better when books are difficult to read, but interesting than when books are simple but boring. Learning skills develop out of wanting to read a certain book as often as they do out of mastering the skills required to sound out the words in the book.

### Reading Goals

A good way to articulate your goals for a reading program is to select half a dozen books that your students cannot now deal with but that you would like them to be able to read by the end of the year. I hoped, for example, that by the end of the year all of my first-grade students would be able to read such books as *The Cat in the Hat Comes Back* and *Green Eggs and Ham* by Dr. Seuss (Beginner Books, Random House), *Monster Goes to the Zoo* by Ellen Blance and Ann Cook (Bowmar), *Anansi the Spider*, retold and illustrated by Gerald McDermott (Holt, Rinehart), *What's Inside* by May Garelick, and *The Bigger Giant* by Nancy Green (both Scholastic.)

There is quite a range of difficulty even among these six books. However, I feel that students who can deal with unfamiliar books on the level of any of these are doing well enough at the end of the first grade. Not every student will do as well as I hope, and some will do much better than I imagined possible. In any case, by setting an objective I have some sense of what I would like to see happen, and I can share it with others.

The way I find out whether or not the students in my class have achieved my objectives is quite simple: I ask them to read. They can tell how they're doing, too, because I show them the kinds of books I hope they can deal with by the end of the year. By talking with the children as we go along, I can find out what problems they face in trying to read those books. In this way my students help me design programs for them.

### Overall to Specific

Your overall behavioral objectives can be made specific by developing monthly or weekly goals for your work in the classroom. These goals have to be planned tentatively, though, and rethought weekly since unexpected things happen and a teacher who cares about how young people learn has to follow their lead. If even the best of plans are held too rigidly without regard for what students are thinking and feeling, it is possible to end up with the sad situation in which little is thought and what is felt is concealed. Even if you hold to the same overall goals, you are likely to find it necessary to redesign your strategy every week. The box in the chart shows two examples of specific weekly goals that we felt are sensible to plan, using the same simple form as that for the overall objectives.

It has been my experience that the more short-range objectives I set for myself the more often they have to be revised to conform to the actual responses of my students. It is possible to set objectives so finely that they seem to account for every second you are with your students. At that point the objectives can squeeze out teaching so that little remains except stating a small skill and then testing to see whether your students have listened well enough to pass a test that is supposed to

## Student Reading Profile

| | Skills | Confidence | Strategy | UNDERSTANDING | | PHYSICAL CONDITIONING | |
| --- | --- | --- | --- | --- | --- | --- | --- |
| | | | | Street Understanding | Book Understanding | Speed | Stamina |
| Beginning | 1. Knowing print<br>2. Known words<br>3. Words that con-<br>nect and words<br>that place<br>4. Alphabet<br>5. Sounds and<br>combinations<br>of sounds<br>6. Simple sentences | none<br>not much<br>enough | Panics<br>Evades<br>Copes<br>Deals | Not at all<br>With problems<br>OK | Not at all<br>With problems<br>OK | Very slow<br>Slow<br>OK<br>Speed freak | No stamina<br>Problems w/<br>stamina<br>OK<br>Stamina freak |
| Not Bad | 1. Combinations<br>of sounds<br>2. Complicated<br>words<br>3. Complex sen-<br>tences<br>4. Everyday reading<br>5. Paragraphs and<br>stories | none<br>not much<br>enough | Panics<br>Evades<br>Copes<br>Deals | Not at all<br>With problems<br>OK | Not at all<br>With problems<br>OK | Very slow<br>Slow<br>OK<br>Speed freak | No stamina<br>Problems w/<br>stamina<br>OK<br>Stamina freak |
| With Ease | 1. Unfamiliar words<br>2. Different forms<br>of writing<br>3. Voice<br>4. Test taking | none<br>not much<br>enough | Panics<br>Evades<br>Copes<br>Deals | Not at all<br>With problems<br>OK | Not at all<br>With problems<br>OK | Very slow<br>Slow<br>OK<br>Speed freak | No stamina<br>Problems w/<br>stamina<br>OK<br>Stamina freak |
| Complex | 1. Knowing about<br>language<br>2. Special uses of<br>words<br>3. Special languages<br>4. Critical analysis | none<br>not much<br>enough | Panics<br>Evades<br>Copes<br>Deals | Not at all<br>With problems<br>OK | Not at all<br>With problems<br>OK | Very slow<br>Slow<br>OK<br>Speed freak | No stamina<br>Problems w/<br>stamina<br>OK<br>Stamina freak |

A reading profile states in the simplest language possible what reading skills a student has and might need over the course of the year. It uses no numbers, no educational jargon, no standardized tests. It is behavioral in the sense that it refers to skills and not to standardized measures or levels. Most experienced teachers can make up their own. The above example of such a profile is from my book *Reading, How to* (Bantam) [Copyright © 1973]. In the skills column "√" stands for "knows it," "0" stands for "has some mastery" and "x" stands for "has no idea."

guarantee that they have mastered that skill. Where is the time for exploration, discovery, practive, play—for learning?

## Keeping Goals Simple and Sensible

Basically, behavioral objectives represent simple and often sensible ideas that most teachers either have used or would readily use if it would make their work with their students more effective. What my friend and many teachers are experiencing is that the articulation of goals, which is a good idea, can turn into a complex system that prevents them from teaching.

However, taking what is valuable of the behavioral objectives concept can help us to clarify our ideas and goals and in so doing help us help our students. My friend has begun to articulate her own behavioral objectives and is ready to make a case for them.

# C
# *Stamina, Patience, and Pacing*

How to pace yourself over a teaching year and make the last days of the semester the fullest.

*T*here are times of the year when teachers and students get tired of each other and the routines and rituals they have fallen into. This fatigue is indicted in many different ways.

Teachers take their excused absences more frequently during these times. Students and teachers know exactly how many days there are to the next holiday. And everybody remembers what happened on Monday and Friday but forgets the content of Tuesday, Wednesday, and Thursday. Weekends seem shorter and weeks longer. Even the most interesting subjects seem flavorless, and the most open classrooms oppressive.

I generally experience my doldrums in late November, early February, and mid-May. It is almost as if the cycles in my classroom life come to an end at three-month intervals, and then the students and I need time off from each other to think about what has happened between us and reflect upon what was learned or felt in the classroom.

I also experience times of quietude and aimlessness with my students after we have done something particularly exciting or important. For example, when we master a play, or think through a math problem that has stumped us for weeks, or manage to resolve a particularly delicate group conflict, or create a piece of work that moves us all, we are reluctant to talk about the experience or to come together immediately to begin new work.

I know when something moves me particularly, I want time to savor it, think about it, hold it in my mind and imagination. My students have told me that they feel the same way.

In most classrooms, however, there is no time to reflect or hold at a particular point and drift for awhile. There is little time to celebrate communal achievement or discuss and respect boredom and weariness. Yet it seems to me that it is crucial that the rhythm of the school year be adjusted to the organic rhythms of individual classes. Learning cannot be parcelled out evenly over all the days of the year, and every day cannot be expected to contain the same amount of material to be covered. There must be peaks and valleys, variations in the quality and quantity of work done at different times.

It is hardly possible to go along studying history or doing math at the same steady pace throughout a school year without destroying the excitement the subjects can have for students or making rote memorization take the place of understanding. A particularly keen historical insight or an elegant line of mathematical reasoning ought to be savored. Sometimes it takes time to understand a particular concept and that means pausing for awhile and thinking it through.

There are times when students will do dull regular work in order to master a subject or a skill. I have seen students practicing on musical instruments, or drawing or writing for two hours at a time, just trying to get things right. However, even the most dedicated musician or writer grows weary of work or practice at times and needs a rest, a change of pace. The same is true for young people.

I remember a particular lull period. My students and I ended a number of projects. We finished a theater piece we were working on, sent our magazine to press and managed to get through a particularly difficult part of set theory. Some of the continuing quarrels in the class seemed to have been resolved temporarily. And we were tired. We didn't want to start on new things and there were no holidays in sight.

I don't really know what to do in cases like this and often feel like calling in absent. I wish I could call off school for a couple of days for all of us. Then we could have a chance to absorb what we have done and be able to be relaxed and refreshed when we meet again. But I can't: There is compulsory attendance and the students might be arrested for truancy. Besides, most of the parents want their children in school every day.

### To Picnic, Walk or Talk

The only thing I can think of is going to the park with my class for several days. We could picnic, talk, walk, play, avoid everything having to do with school, and spend time refreshing ourselves. There is no justification for our doing this other than that we need and care to do it right now.

As things are presently structured in the public schools, however, it is impossible to set aside time to relax and change the daily routine of life. Trips have to be justified; even walks around the block have to be described in terms of educational objectives.

People can't do things simply because they may seem to be nice or interesting things to do, or because there is a need for a change of pace. Yet we have to relax, to celebrate something, to do things because they seem pleasant or interesting. It is as valuable for students and teachers to spend a nice day together walking and talking, as it is for them to go to a special exhibit and see how people in another world live.

Often there is as much a need for a change of scene in the classroom as for a change of pace. The decor of the room may become boring after awhile or it might reflect activities no longer relevant to the students' interests. I know that I feel the same way about the decor of my study. Every once in awhile, usually after I feel that a period in my life or writing has passed, I feel an urge to change the environment and start anew.

The same thing happens in the classroom. There are times when the students begin to complain about the room. It seems dull, the posters and work they have put up are no longer interesting, the desks or chairs or cushions or couches seem uncomfortable.

At these times of special boredom, I have found that one thing that worked was a ritual housecleaning. The students and I would take the classroom apart, throw out all the old posters and decorations, move all the chairs and tables out of the room and then begin again. A day of housecleaning, followed by a day of rebuilding the classroom environment, almost always served to renew our interest in the room and in our lives together.

There is a need for constant renewal of interest and energy in the classroom. And there is a need for time to rest and do nothing. When young people work hard at learning (and it often happens if they are free to learn what they care to know), there are times when they are exhausted. There are other times when they are too filled with what they have just learned to be ready to move immediately on to something else, something new.

It is crucial that teachers respect the personal and often private, nature of learning and enable their students to take the time to think and reflect upon what they are doing. Time can't be objectified and students required to learn on schedule. Nor can space be set once and for all without regard for the comfort of people who live within it. The classroom must be responsive to the pace with which students learn and to their need for a rich and changing environment. There also have to be times when, for the sake of our sanity, we simply have fun and do somewhat crazy things together.

Bill Matthews, a friend who teaches in a small school about 20 miles from where I live, mentioned casually the other day that it was egg wrapping time of the year. Since I had no idea of what he was talking about he elaborated. Egg wrapping consists of giving the students in his class one egg each and challenging them to wrap the eggs in such a way that they will not break when dropped from the roof of the school. Bill said the packages were due the next day and that he would drop them from the roof during lunchtime.

Bill also explained that egg wrapping was part of his curriculum on construction and the strength of materials, but even more — it was fun. The word "fun" was jarring because I realized how seldom fun seems to be part of teaching these days. Over the past six months I have noticed a growing melancholy in schools and classrooms I have visited. Melancholy is a peculiar state of the soul. The word "melancholy" means black bile which, according to the ancient Greeks, is supposed to produce sustained states of depression. A sustained state of depression is a good way to describe the current mood of too many people in the public schools these days. This seems to be the consequence of the drying up of funds, the effect of small raises in the face of inflation, and a general sense of not being appreciated by the public. While trying to restore public confidence and fight for decent salary adjustments, we also have to throw off this depression and find ways of having fun with our students in the classroom if we are to take any pleasure in our work. Here are some suggestions of things you might do during the last two months of the school year that are fun as well as instructional:

1. Building grand models of cities of the future in one corner of the room can be fun. Collect boxes of wood, metal and cloth scraps, as well as other miscellaneous junk; name a city or planet; and then break up into building teams of four or five students. Each team is responsible for some aspect of the construction and has to coordinate their work with the work of other teams. For example, one team can build a port, another an airport, another a residential community, another schools and other public buildings, or an amusement park. The whole has to be paved, and roads and street layouts have to be created. The experience of building a city can fit into many areas of the curriculum and can be justified in many different ways. However, the fun it can provide a group is, for me, its main justification.

2. Finding a way to simulate traveling thousands of miles is another source of fun. I got this idea from Ron Jones. At the Center for the Handicapped there is an exercise bike. Ron put up a large map of the United States and suggested that his students try to bike their way to New York on the exercise bike and chart their trip on the map. 3,000 miles and several weeks later the group had biked the distance from San Francisco to New York without leaving their room. They had a "Welcome to New York" party on arrival. If you can bring an exercise bike to class (one that had a pedometer) you can go anywhere you imagine, plot

your trip, and even study what you encounter on the way. If you can't find an exercise bike then it might be fun to invent a treadmill, or to take measured walks that would achieve the same purpose.

3. Creating musical instruments and composing and performing music is another possibility. With a number of bottles, slats of wood hung from the ceiling, tin cans, bells, knives, forks, spoons, and other invented instruments, it is possible to make a class orchestra. I've found that students are sometimes shy about making music together on an informal and slightly silly basis. One way to overcome this is to have everyone take something that can make a sound and make a sound with it. Then you take an instrument yourself and set up a rhythm and invite people to join in. After a while everyone will be playing and, hopefully, will feel that no one is judging their musical competency or trying to give them a grade. If you persist and play together several times a week, patterns will develop and the group will get to know each other musically and develop themes and variations of it, some of which will be musically interesting and all of which should provide fun for the class.

4. Clowning is another thing that can be done quite easily. There are some basic clown tricks like falling and seeming to slap or be slapped by another clown. There are also basic clown faces: exaggerated smiles or crying faces, big noses or ears. Within those basic types there are unlimited variations. Students can create clown characters for themselves, dress up as clowns, practice routines with each other. They can try to be sad and funny, or clumsy, or overconfident, or bumbling. They can also study professional clowns if you are lucky enough to have a circus in town or have access to circus films. Ringling Bros. Barnum and Bailey Circus also has an education division and will be able to provide you with material to help the development of clown characters. Books on Harlequin and Punch and Judy will also be helpful.

5. Clowning can be extended in a number of way. A clown puppet show or a Punch and Judy show can be developed and produced by students. Juggling, tumbling, and other forms of acrobatics can be added and you should develop your own circus and perform for other classes. In my community a mime teacher, Sandi Zeig, taught a circus class for elementary school students and after several months the students put on a performance of what they called Circus Minimus, a tiny circus. There is no reason why time can't be found to make your own version of Circus Minimus.

6. Most of these suggestions for having fun in the classroom involve the arts. It is no accident that learning and fun are most successfully merged through the arts. I believe that the arts are basic skills that are

too often neglected or treated as frills in the schools. If we could put the arts in as central a place as the so-called, other basics not only would teaching be more fun, but learning in all areas would benefit. Here are some other arts projects that provide group fun and group learning: doing a large mural on the wall of the school with everyone contributing to the design and having a hand in the painting; developing a mime troupe in which students of all ages plan a silent performance having a common theme, such as the growth of a person from birth to death or the development and use of life-giving magical powers; and, finally, developing a teacher acting troupe to perform for the students and show them that there is life in the staff.

What we need most now is to reaffirm for ourselves and the parents that we work for the joy of teaching. All the behavioral objectives and special programs in the world will not recreate the faith and belief in public schools and teachers that can be easily won by displaying joy in teaching.

# D
# Doing the Unexpected

This last section is on the need we all feel to be a bit crazy, to change the daily routine, and to do things that are different and fun in school every once in a while.

*I*t's hard to know what will excite children. Sometimes the most carefully planned lessons fall flat. At others times a casual comment sets off ideas and associations and releases energy that you didn't know existed.

One day, during my first year of teaching, I came upon a fascinating magazine picture of a very big fish eating a tiny fish. The picture was captioned "Big fish eat little fish." Though it had no relationship to anything that was happening in my classroom at that time, I cut the picture out, took it to school and stapled it to the bulletin board in the back of the room. Then I forgot about it.

One day about a week later there was some commotion in the back of the room. A student had discovered the picture and called her friends over to look. Feeling excitement in the room, I went to see what was going on. One student turned to me and, in an intense and somewhat puzzled voice, demanded "Where did this come from?" I replied that I put it there. Another student asked why.

### Surprise

It occurred to me then that students are accustomed to thinking that everything teachers do in the classroom is predictable and has learning goals. The idea of introducing something just to see what will happen is foreign.

Yet, the discussions emerging from the "Big fish eat little fish" picture were as interesting as anything that happened that year. One student related it to the problems he was having with some schoolyard bullies. Another told how what the picture showed was similar to what her father was always saying: that his life was "dog eat dog." One of the smallest boys said that to keep big fish from eating little fish, all you needed were some big friends.

Ever since I put that picture up I've been gathering materials (pictures, articles, packages, catalogs) that look interesting, even if they have no direct relationship to something I'm doing with my students or planning for them. I keep many of them in an "image file," a cardboard filing cabinet that is organized with folders with titles like, "faces," "parts of the body," "people playing," "misery," "joy," "pets," "proverbs," "products," "type faces," "love scenes," "maps," "graphs," "headlines," "movie ads," "cars," "superheroes" and "magic tricks."

The images in my file have two functions: to provide visual material to make the usual curriculum more interesting and to keep a steady flow of new and unexpected material on the walls of the classroom. Some of the pictures I put up are never noticed; some lead to interesting discussions; other shift the overall content and flow of our work.

For example, I once posted a picture of the funeral of several fire fighters who were killed fighting a fire. Several students noticed the picture right away and asked to discuss the fire and the dangers of fire fighting. Later, another student talked about his aunt's funeral. The subject of death had been brought up for the first time. Everybody wanted to discuss dying, the possibility of life after death, the way people bury and honor the dead, as well as the things that lead to death.

### Student Input

One year a number of students asked me if they could have a part of the bulletin board to put up pictures and other things that they would like to share. I was delighted, of course, and a whole new spirit entered the room. Students brought in clippings from local papers, ads for songs, church and political handouts, wedding invitations and so on. The effects of this sharing were so positive that since then I've included a student bulletin board in every class, no matter what the age of my students.

Introducing the unexpected into the classroom is one way of experimenting with learning, and I've found teaching to be interesting and effective only when I experiment constantly. We can't simply depend on a set curriculum, knowing we aren't aware of everything that interests our students and that every group of students has a different constellation of interests.

Teachers are the innovators and creators in education. The best material comes out of the work we do in the classroom because there is a need, a gap, or boredom. Teaching can become dull and uninspiring when we use the materials assigned to us only in the ways that the teacher manuals suggest, without using our own energies to respond to the particular students we have at that time.

The finest innovative materials that exist are teacher created. All the materials reproduced by Ron Jones in *Deschooling Primers* (Zephyros) were sent to him by classroom teachers who developed materials to meet students' needs. (For a free catalog, write to Zephyros, 1201 Stanyan St., San Francisco, CA 94117.) What we see at the Center for Open Learning and Teaching continues to reinforce our faith in teacher-created materials.

### Preparation and Evaluation

Developing material that works with young people is not merely a matter of doing the unexpected and being open to what students do with new ideas and materials. It also requires preparation and evaluation.

I have found it necessary to set up a small, home workshop that includes everything I need to plan, create and reevaluate what I do in my classroom. I've tried to do some of this in the teachers' workrooms in schools where I've taught, but it doesn't work. I need the time and distance that even a small corner at home provides.

All I need in my workshop are my image file, paper, duplicating masters, felt-tip pens, glue, scissors, a stapler, and simple tools to make things out of wood. I also store games and keep puzzle and alphabet books, and books of math and reading games. I keep a folder for each student to keep track of his or her achievements and needs and jot down ideas that might be enriching for that child. I might experiment with a new game, research something that a student has expressed interest in, make a poster or pick an image to post on the bulletin board.

During these times of thinking and making things myself, the work of teaching takes on another creative dimension for me. Both the creativity in working with students and this invention and design make teaching an unending source of challenge.

Here are a few resources that can help you put a working place together:

*How to Make Your Own Educational Materials* by Cynthia Brown and Ray Nitta ($4.00 from P.O. Box 242, Point Arena, CA 95468). This book lists tools, describes storage space, and has information on bookbinding, making puzzles and games and musical instruments.
*Bookcraft* by Annette Hollander (van Nostrand/Reinhold) $5.95. A useful step by step description of how to make attractive books, folders, and binders, with a list of simple and useful tools.
*Printing It* by Clifford Burke (Wingbow Press, $3.00 available from Book People, 2940 Seventh St., Berkeley, CA 94710) A clear and useful book on how to do

layout and design with a description of tools and working space. Even if you only intend to do simple mimeographed papers and books this is invaluable. It also can help you understand how to do printing with your students.

*How to Work With Tools and Wood* ed. by Robert Campbell and N. H. Mager (Pocket Books, $1.25) A good inexpensive volume which shows how to use and care for woodworking tools, as well as talking about which tools are best for particular projects.

My book *Math, Writing and Games* (New York Review, Vintage) has a section on setting up a game-making center in the classroom. Actually the gamemaking center I used in my class was designed to be an extended version of the one I used at home to make games for my classroom and I think it would be useful to take a look at that part of the book and scale things down to the space you have available.